Rewired for Resilience:

The Neurosomatic Path to Healing, Embodiment, and Transformation

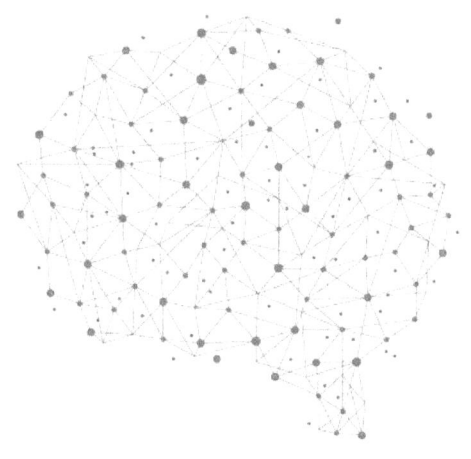

By: Dr. Deilen Michelle Villegas, Ph.D.

Copyright © 2025 Dr. Deilen Michelle Villegas, Ph.D.
All Rights Reserved.

No part of this publication may be reproduced, distributed, or transmitted in any form or by any means—including photocopying, recording, or other electronic or mechanical methods—without the prior written permission of the author, except in the case of brief quotations embodied in critical reviews and certain other noncommercial uses permitted by copyright law.

For permission requests, write to the publisher at:
The Shamanic Goddess, LLC
Charlotte, North Carolina
www.DrDeilenMVillegas.com
Dr.Deilen.Villegas@gmail.com

This book is intended for educational purposes only and is not a substitute for professional medical or mental health advice. The author and publisher disclaim any liability arising directly or indirectly from the use of the information contained in this book. Readers are encouraged to consult qualified professionals regarding personal health and wellness decisions.

Book Title: Rewired for Resilience: The Neurosomatic Path to
Healing, Embodiment, and Transformation
Author: Dr. Deilen Michelle Villegas, Ph.D.
Publisher: The Shamanic Goddess, LLC
Cover and Interior Design: The Shamanic Goddess, LLC
ISBN: 978-1-969550-40-9
First Edition: 2025
Printed in the United States of America

Book Objective

This volume aims to advance practitioner and client understanding of the nervous system as both a site of trauma imprinting and a portal for transformation. Grounded in emerging research from neuroscience, somatic psychology, and embodied therapeutic practice, this book introduces and contextualizes the principles of **Neurosomatic Intelligence (NSI)** as a comprehensive, integrative framework for healing.

Its primary objectives are:

- To educate clinicians, coaches, mental health practitioners, and trauma survivors on the neurobiological and behavioral mechanisms underlying trauma, dysregulation, and adaptation;

- To illustrate how survival-based responses, such as dissociation, hypervigilance, collapse, and compulsive behaviors, are not pathological, but protective nervous system strategies;

- To offer somatically-based, evidence-informed interventions for emotional regulation, stress recovery, and capacity building;

- To support sustainable healing through practical applications of neuroplasticity, interoception, and co-regulation in both therapeutic and lived settings.

Rather than centering symptom suppression or cognitive override, this text emphasizes bottom-up change, restoring relationship with the body as an intelligent partner in the healing process. Each chapter contributes to a cumulative understanding of how practitioners and clients can work in partnership with the nervous system to foster resilience, embodiment, and self-authored transformation.

ABOUT THE AUTHOR

Dr. Deilen Michelle Villegas, Ph.D., is a Board-Certified Holistic Health and Wellness Practitioner, Clinical Mental Health Counselor, Neurosomatic and Psychosomatic Educator, Certified Clinical Sexologist, and internationally recognized Trauma Specialist. She is the visionary founder and CEO of *The Shamanic Goddess, LLC*, where she integrates cutting-edge neuroscience, ancient healing wisdom, and trauma-informed care to help individuals reclaim their power, purpose, and physiological safety.

With over 18 years of experience across Internal Medicine, Pediatrics, OB/GYN, Oncology, Triage, and Behavioral Health, Dr. Villegas brings a uniquely interdisciplinary lens to holistic care. Her academic foundation includes a Ph.D. in Organizational Leadership, an M.Sc. in Complementary and Integrative Medicine, an M.A. in Clinical Mental Health Counseling, and a Doctorate in Natural Medicine. She is also a certified practitioner of Neurosomatic Intelligence (NSI), combining polyvagal-informed, somatic-based interventions with culturally attuned healing models.

A mother, community healer, educator, and advocate, Dr. Villegas is dedicated to decolonizing wellness and amplifying access to trauma-informed, body-centered healing in underserved and BIPOC communities. Her work bridges science and spirituality, guiding clients and clinicians alike into deeper embodiment, emotional regulation, and nervous system transformation.

She is the author of multiple works exploring trauma, intergenerational healing, somatic intelligence, and identity reclamation. With humility and fierce compassion, she continues to stand at the intersection of medicine, mysticism, and mentorship, offering tools, language, and sanctuary for those on the journey from survival to sovereignty.

Table Of Contents

Book Objective
About The Author
Introduction: The Nervous System Is The Portal to Change

Section I: Foundations of The Neurosomatic Model
1. Foundations of Nervous System Work
2. The Neurology of Beliefs, Identity, and Bias
3. Emotional Regulation and Somatic Expression

Section II: Patterns of Protection and Dysregulation
4. Freeze, Dissociation, and Survival Based Shutdown
5. Anxiety and Overwhelm
6. Anger, Reactivity, and Self-Sabotage
7. Fawn Response, Attachment, and Boundaries

Section III: Reconnection and Repatterning
8. Co-Regulation and Relational Healing
9. Building Somatic Resilience and Emotional Agility
10. Body Relationship, Eating, and Gut Health
11. Peace, Rest, and Sleep Recovery
12. Play, Joy, and Nervous System Expansion

Section IV: Integration and Transformation
13. Inner Critic, Shame, and Self-Compassion
14. Grief, Identity, and Integration
15. HabitChange and Addictive Behaviors
16. Visibility, Presence, and Connection

Conclusion: The Body Remembers…and Rewires
Practitioners Afterword: Reclaiming the Embodies Self

Appendices:
- Glossary of Terms
- Neurosomatic Intelligence (NSI) Principles
- Practitioner Tools & Protocols

- Nervous System States Chart
- Daily Practice Templates
- Recommended Reading & Resources
- Client Consent & Safety Practices
- Acknowledgments

INTRODUCTION

The Nervous System Is the Portal to Change

Why We Must Begin with the Body

For too long, the healing journey has been approached from the top down; attempting to think, talk, and analyze our way out of pain. Yet the truth, backed by decades of neuroscience and trauma research, is this: the body remembers what the mind forgets. The nervous system, not the intellect, is the true gatekeeper of safety, identity, and transformation.

In a world grappling with anxiety, disconnection, burnout, and chronic dysregulation, we are witnessing a paradigm shift. No longer is emotional resilience considered a trait; it is now understood as a trainable, physiological state. At the core of this evolution is **Neurosomatic Intelligence (NSI)**: a science-backed, somatically informed, trauma-aware framework that helps individuals, clinicians, and practitioners regulate and rewire their nervous systems.

This book was created to bridge what modern neuroscience is uncovering with what ancient healing traditions have always known: that true healing is a full-body process. Through this work, we are not just chasing symptom relief; we are creating internal conditions for lasting safety, sustainable change, and soul-level embodiment.

The Nervous System: Our Hidden Operating System

Our nervous system interprets every experience and dictates our responses to the world. It determines whether we freeze or fight, shut down or speak up, lash out or lean in. This internal system, consisting of the brain, spinal cord, vagus nerve, and peripheral network, is constantly evaluating one question: *Am I safe?*

According to Dr. Stephen Porges' **Polyvagal Theory**, the nervous system subconsciously scans our environment through "neuroception," evaluating cues of safety and danger even before the brain becomes consciously aware of them (Porges, 2011). This biological process explains why traditional talk therapy often falls short for trauma survivors: if the body doesn't feel safe, the mind cannot engage.

By learning to regulate the nervous system through somatic tools, we can begin to rewire not just our behaviors but the underlying neurobiology that drives them.

From Trauma to Transformation

Trauma is not what happens to us; it's what happens inside us as a result of what happened to us. When we experience a threat that overwhelms our capacity to cope, our nervous system stores the event somatically. As Dr. Bessel van der Kolk writes in *The Body Keeps the Score*, traumatic memories are encoded in the body as sensations, postures, and stress patterns, not just thoughts (van der Kolk, 2014).

Neurosomatic Intelligence provides a roadmap for integrating these fragmented patterns through body-based protocols, neuroplastic training, and trauma-informed strategies. This approach doesn't just help you "cope"; it teaches you how to **regulate**, **restore**, and **reclaim** your nervous system from the inside out.

The Need for an Embodied, Evidence-Based Approach

While somatic practices have existed for centuries, modern neuroscience is finally catching up to validate their power. Research now confirms:

- Mind-body practices like meditation, breathwork, and vagus nerve stimulation improve autonomic regulation and reduce inflammatory markers (Gerritsen & Band, 2018; Tracey, 2002).

- Emotional dysregulation is strongly correlated with altered amygdala and prefrontal cortex function, areas that can be retrained through neuroplasticity (Etkin et al., 2015).

- Shame, trauma, and chronic stress impair the body's ability to down-regulate, contributing to autoimmune conditions, anxiety, and pain (Sapolsky, 2004; Lanius et al., 2010).

This book grounds every chapter in peer-reviewed literature and clinical research, making it accessible to practitioners while still resonating with everyday readers. You'll find case studies, guided tools, nervous system maps, and somatic exercises to bring this science to life.

The NSI Framework: A New Path to Healing

The chapters ahead are built on the 12 core modules of the Neurosomatic Intelligence curriculum. Each one targets a specific area of nervous system function and dysregulation, ranging from emotional regulation to addiction, embodiment to habit change, insomnia to visibility. Whether you're a clinician, a coach, or someone navigating your own healing, this book offers a practical blueprint for nervous system resilience.

Here's what to expect:

Section	Focus	Goal
Part I	Foundations of	Understand neuroplasticity, safety, and regulation

	NSI	
Part II	Trauma & Dysregulation	Repattern chronic stress responses and survival strategies
Part III	Reconnection & Rewiring	Restore presence, purpose, and parasympathetic access
Part IV	Integration	Create long-term transformation and embodied self-leadership

Each module will offer:
- A breakdown of key scientific concepts

- Somatic and neurosomatic tools for practice

- Real-life application stories and strategies

- References to leading-edge neuroscience and trauma research

An Invitation to Embody Change

Healing is not linear. It is cyclical, layered, and deeply personal. But it is also **possible**. The nervous system is capable of profound repair when given the right conditions, and you are capable of creating those conditions.

This book is more than information. It is an invitation:

To stop blaming yourself for survival patterns.
To stop bypassing the body for the sake of the mind.
To stop waiting for safety and begin cultivating it, cell by cell, breath by breath.

You are not broken. You are wired for survival. And now, you're being called to rewire for something greater: peace, power, and purpose.

Welcome to the work. Let's begin.

Selected References
- Etkin, A., Büchel, C., & Gross, J. J. (2015). The neural bases of emotion regulation. *Nature Reviews Neuroscience*, 16(11), 693–700.

- **Gerritsen, R. J., & Band, G. P. (2018).** Breath of life: The respiratory vagal stimulation model of contemplative activity. *Frontiers in Human Neuroscience*, 12, 397.

- **Lanius, R. A., Frewen, P. A., Vermetten, E., & Yehuda, R.** (2010). Fear conditioning and early life vulnerabilities: Two distinct pathways of emotional dysregulation and brain dysfunction in PTSD. *European Journal of Psychotraumatology*, 1(1), 5467.

- **Porges, S. W. (2011).** *The Polyvagal Theory: Neurophysiological foundations of emotions, attachment, communication, and self-regulation.* W. W. Norton & Company.

- **Sapolsky, R. M. (2004).** *Why zebras don't get ulcers: The acclaimed guide to stress, stress-related diseases, and coping.* Holt Paperbacks.

- **Tracey, K. J. (2002).** The inflammatory reflex. *Nature*, 420(6917), 853–859.

- **van der Kolk, B. A. (2014).** *The Body Keeps the Score: Brain, mind, and body in the healing of trauma.* Viking.

SECTION I: FOUNDATIONS OF THE NEUROSOMATIC MODEL

CHAPTER 1

Foundations of Nervous System Work

The Nervous System as the Core Operating System

The human nervous system serves as the body's master interpreter and regulatory hub. It continuously scans, filters, and organizes sensory data, emotional stimuli, and internal physiological signals, determining how we perceive our environment, relate to others, and recover from stressors. Every sensation, thought, emotion, and behavior is influenced, if not governed, by this intricate system of neural circuits and feedback loops.

When the nervous system is balanced and well-regulated, it promotes adaptive functioning: clarity of thought, emotional resilience, relational attunement, and physiological equilibrium. However, when it becomes dysregulated, often as a result of trauma, chronic stress, systemic oppression, or early developmental disruption, this equilibrium is disrupted. The body may interpret neutral cues as threats, emotions become dysregulated, and survival strategies like hypervigilance, shutdown, or dissociation become the norm. In these states, our capacity to feel safe, connected, and empowered is diminished at the root level.

Understanding and working directly with this system is not optional for deep, sustainable healing; it is essential. As emerging research in **polyvagal theory** (Porges, 2011), **affective neuroscience** (Davidson & Begley, 2012), and **trauma-informed care** (van der Kolk, 2014) continues to reveal, the nervous system is not merely involved in healing; it is where healing begins. When we regulate the body, we shift the brain. When we restore physiological safety, we restore the possibility of transformation.

Nervous System Inputs and Outputs: Understanding the Circuit

The human nervous system is not a passive observer of reality; it is an active, adaptive circuit that continuously receives, interprets, and responds to information from both the external environment and the body's internal state. Every second, millions of signals are processed through intricate neural pathways, creating a living feedback loop that determines how we feel, think, and act. This ongoing exchange of information is not random; it is governed by the nervous system's primary imperative: **to assess safety, respond to threat, and maintain balance**.

From a neuroscience perspective, this is often described as an **input-output system**—a dynamic loop in which incoming sensory and internal data are translated into physiological, emotional, and behavioral responses. This circuit determines not only whether we feel calm, connected, and capable, but also whether we shift into protective survival states such as fight, flight, freeze, or fawn.

Inputs: How the Nervous System Reads the World

Inputs are the raw data points, the sensory and internal cues, that inform the nervous system's neuroceptive process (Porges, 2011). They serve as the "early warning system" for detecting safety, danger, or life threat. Importantly, this process operates below conscious awareness, meaning we often respond to perceived danger before our thinking brain has even registered what is happening.

Key categories of nervous system inputs include:

1. **Sensory Information**
   Our five primary senses – vision, hearing, touch, smell, and taste – form the foundation of environmental perception. The brightness of a room, the pitch of a voice, the texture of clothing, or the scent of a familiar meal can either cue safety or signal potential danger. Sensory input is not neutral; it is filtered through our past experiences and shaped by learned associations.

2. **Interoceptive Signals**
   Interoception refers to the body's awareness of its internal state, including signals such as heartbeat, respiration, hunger, satiety, temperature, and visceral sensations like nausea or "butterflies" in the stomach (Craig, 2002). A healthy interoceptive system allows for nuanced self-regulation—knowing when to rest, eat, hydrate, or move. In a dysregulated system, these signals may be misinterpreted as signs of danger (e.g., interpreting an elevated heart rate from exercise as a panic attack).

3. **Social and Environmental Cues**
   Humans are deeply social beings, wired for connection. Facial expressions, eye contact, body posture, tone of voice, and even micro-rhythms in conversation provide powerful cues that the nervous system uses to determine whether we are in a safe or threatening social context. This subconscious scanning—**neuroception**—is central to the Polyvagal Theory (Porges, 2011) and explains why the presence of a calm, attuned person can settle our own physiology, while subtle signs of tension can activate defense states.

Outputs: How the Nervous System Responds

Once inputs are received and processed, the nervous system generates outputs—physiological, emotional, and behavioral responses that aim to protect, restore, or maintain equilibrium. These outputs are not random reactions; they are adaptive survival strategies honed through both personal history and evolutionary necessity.

1. **Physiological Responses**
   Shifts in heart rate, respiratory patterns, muscle tone, digestion, and hormonal release prepare the body for the demands of the perceived situation. For example, sympathetic activation increases heart rate and blood flow to muscles during threat, while parasympathetic dominance slows heart rate and supports digestion in safe states.

2. **Emotional Expressions**
   Emotions serve as both internal signals and social communication tools. Crying may signal distress and seek connection, laughter may reinforce social bonds, and anger may serve to protect boundaries. These expressions are often shaped by both biology and cultural conditioning.

3. **Behavioral Responses**
   The body's actions—whether approaching, withdrawing, freezing, fawning, confronting, or speaking—are the visible manifestations of nervous system state. They are not merely "choices" in the cognitive sense but are deeply informed by the autonomic state at any given moment.

The Circuit in Regulation vs. Dysregulation

In a **regulated nervous system**, inputs and outputs flow with adaptive precision. Safety cues are recognized as such, threat cues are addressed effectively, and recovery is swift once the challenge passes. This capacity for fluid adjustment is the foundation of **resilience**—the ability to return to baseline after stress.

In a **dysregulated nervous system**, often shaped by trauma, chronic stress, or early adversity, the input-output loop becomes biased toward threat detection. Neutral or even positive inputs may be misinterpreted as dangerous, leading to persistent activation of defensive states such as hypervigilance, shutdown, or dissociation (van der Kolk, 2014; Lanius et al., 2010). Over time, this distorted baseline can lead to physical symptoms (e.g., chronic pain, fatigue, digestive distress), emotional difficulties (e.g., anxiety, irritability, numbness), and relational challenges (e.g., withdrawal, mistrust, conflict).

From Awareness To Intervention

Understanding the nervous system as a **sensory circuit**—not merely a cognitive or emotional entity—is the first step toward embodied healing. Rather than attempting to "think" our way out of distress, we can begin to consciously influence inputs (through breathwork, mindful movement, and sensory anchoring) to create shifts in outputs.

This is the essence of bottom-up regulation: **changing the body's state to change the mind's story.** Over time, consistent practice can rewire the loop so that safety—not threat—becomes the default setting.

> "Every input into your nervous system is a message: you are either safe, or you are not. Healing begins when the messages start to shift."

Clinical Application: Working with Inputs and Outputs

For Practitioners:
When assessing a client's nervous system state, consider both

the **quality of inputs** and the **nature of outputs**. Many clients are not consciously aware of what is triggering dysregulation. Use the following as a framework:

- **Map Inputs:** Invite clients to notice specific sensory, interoceptive, and social cues that reliably shift them toward safety or threat.

- **Trace Outputs:** Identify the physiological, emotional, and behavioral patterns that emerge when those inputs occur.

- **Introduce Regulation Tools:** Begin with low-intensity, accessible practices to influence inputs before addressing higher-intensity triggers.

- **Reinforce Safety Cues:** Use relational presence, predictable session structure, and sensory anchoring to signal safety.

For Readers/Clients:

You can begin to shift your nervous system today by tracking inputs and outputs in real time.

Try This: Input Awareness Exercise

1. **Pause and Scan:** In any moment, notice three things you can see, hear, and feel.

2. **Label the Input:** Are these cues signaling *safety*, *neutrality*, or *threat*?

3. **Notice the Output:** What changes in your breath, posture, muscle tone, or thoughts?

4. **Shift the Input:** Introduce a regulating cue—slow your breath, soften your gaze, place a hand over your

heart, or orient to a calming object in the room.

5. **Recheck:** Notice if and how the output changes.

Nervous System Reset Micro-Practices

- **For Overactivation (Fight/Flight):**

  - Lengthen exhalations to twice the length of inhalations.

  - Orient by looking around the space and naming five objects.

  - Use grounding touch (pressing feet into the floor or holding your own forearms).

- **For Underactivation (Freeze/Shutdown):**

  - Engage gentle movement (shoulder rolls, walking, stretching).

  - Listen to upbeat or rhythmically steady music.

  - Increase sensory input (e.g., holding a textured object or sipping cold water).

Remember: You cannot always control the inputs the world gives you, but you can choose how you engage with them—and that choice can shift the entire output of your nervous system.

References

- **Craig, A. D. (2002).** How do you feel? Interoception: the sense of the physiological condition of the body. *Nature Reviews Neuroscience*, 3(8), 655–666.

- **Lanius, R. A., Frewen, P. A., Vermetten, E., & Yehuda, R. (2010).** Fear conditioning and early life vulnerabilities: Two distinct pathways of emotional dysregulation and brain dysfunction in PTSD. *European Journal of Psychotraumatology*, 1(1), 5467.

- **Porges, S. W. (2011).** *The Polyvagal Theory: Neurophysiological foundations of emotions, attachment, communication, and self-regulation.* W. W. Norton & Company.

- **van der Kolk, B. A. (2014).** *The Body Keeps the Score: Brain, mind, and body in the healing of trauma.* Viking.

Neuroception: Safety Without Awareness

Coined by Dr. Stephen Porges (2011) as a central construct of **Polyvagal Theory**, *neuroception* describes the nervous system's **automatic, non-conscious evaluation** of environmental cues to determine whether a given context is safe, dangerous, or life-threatening.

Unlike *perception*, which involves deliberate, conscious interpretation of sensory data, neuroception functions below the threshold of awareness, operating primarily through **subcortical brain structures**—including the **brainstem, amygdala**, and **insula**—that constantly scan for threat or safety signals. This process is not a choice; it is a **primal survival mechanism** shaped by millions of years of evolution.

How Neuroception Works

Neuroception continuously integrates multiple streams of information, including:

- **Sensory Inputs:** Visual, auditory, tactile, olfactory, and proprioceptive cues.

- **Social & Relational Cues:** Facial expressions, eye gaze, posture, micro-movements, vocal prosody, and speech rhythm.

- **Environmental Conditions:** Lighting, soundscapes, spatial arrangement, and proximity of others.

The **interpretation of these cues** determines whether the nervous system:
   1. **Mobilizes** into **sympathetic arousal** (*fight/flight*)
   2. **Collapses** into **dorsal vagal shutdown** (*freeze*)
   3. **Settles** into **ventral vagal regulation** (*safety, connection, presence*)

This appraisal happens within milliseconds—often before the conscious mind has even registered what's occurring.

When Safety Feels Unsafe

In a healthy system, neuroception accurately distinguishes between safe, neutral, and threatening environments.

However, **unresolved trauma, chronic stress, neglect, or unsafe early environments** can distort this filter.

- **Overactive neuroception**: perceives threat where there is none (e.g., panic during public speaking in a supportive setting).

- **Underactive neuroception**: fails to detect danger when it's present (e.g., staying in harmful relationships).

These distortions result in **protective biological adaptations** such as hypervigilance, withdrawal, numbing, or people-pleasing (*fawning*).

They are **not personality flaws or signs of weakness**—they are **learned survival strategies** hardwired through repeated lived experience.

Example:

An individual with a history of developmental trauma may experience **intense discomfort with eye contact, hugging, or emotional closeness**.

While these experiences might be objectively safe in the present, their nervous system reflexively associates them with abandonment, criticism, or harm—activating protective outputs like avoidance, irritability, or shutdown.

Impact of Distorted Neuroception

When left unaddressed, impaired neuroception can contribute to:

- Chronic anxiety or panic without a clear trigger
- Dissociation and disembodiment
- Difficulty reading social cues or emotional tone
- Emotional volatility or complete withdrawal during conflict
- Relational instability—either deep mistrust or over-dependence

This helps explain why **cognitive-only therapeutic interventions**—such as traditional talk therapy—often reach a plateau with trauma survivors. *Insight alone* does not recalibrate the body's threat detection system.

Recalibrating Neuroception: A Bottom-Up Approach

The encouraging truth is that **neuroception is plastic**—it can be retrained through consistent, safety-focused experiences. Neurosomatic Intelligence (NSI) integrates **bottom-up practices** that work directly with the nervous system to:

- **Activate the Vagus Nerve:** via slow diaphragmatic breathing, vocal toning, humming, or cold exposure.

- **Anchor Somatic Safety:** through grounding touch (hand on heart, holding weighted objects) or bilateral stimulation.

- **Foster Relational Co-Regulation:** practicing connection with emotionally attuned, non-judgmental others.

- **Curate Calming Environments:** adjusting lighting, color schemes, sounds, and spatial layouts to reduce sensory threat.

Over time, repeated safe experiences help **reshape the neuroceptive lens**, allowing individuals to:

- Accurately detect safety when it's present

- Build tolerance for deeper connection and stillness

- Experience vulnerability without overwhelm

Key Takeaway:

"We cannot think our way into safety. We must practice it, breathe it, and embody it—until safety feels familiar again."

References

- **Porges, S. W. (2011).** *The Polyvagal Theory: Neurophysiological foundations of emotions, attachment, communication, and self-regulation.* W. W. Norton &

Company.

- **Dana, D. (2018).** *The Polyvagal Theory in Therapy: Engaging the rhythm of regulation.* W. W. Norton & Company.

- **Schore, A. N. (2003).** *Affect Dysregulation and Disorders of the Self.* W. W. Norton & Company.

- **Ogden, P., Minton, K., & Pain, C. (2006).** *Trauma and the Body: A sensorimotor approach to psychotherapy.* W. W. Norton & Company.

Neuroplasticity: The Brain's Power to Change

One of the most empowering discoveries in neuroscience over the past several decades is that the brain—and by extension, the nervous system—is not hardwired or fixed. It is inherently adaptable. This capacity for change is known as **neuroplasticity**: the brain's ability to reorganize its structure, function, and connections in response to experience, repetition, learning, and even injury (Doidge, 2007; Kolb & Whishaw, 2009).

Neuroplasticity is not limited to childhood, as once believed. Adult brains retain the ability to **generate new neural pathways** and **rewire existing ones**, particularly when supported by focused attention, somatic engagement, emotional safety, and deliberate practice (Siegel, 2020). This is especially relevant for trauma recovery, emotional regulation, and behavioral transformation.

From Reaction to Regulation

Every time we respond to a trigger with awareness and regulate instead of react, we interrupt the old neural pathway and begin laying down a new one. Through **repetition, safety, and somatic engagement**, the nervous system learns that it no longer needs to default to protection and can instead build capacity for presence and flexibility.

Neurosomatic Intelligence (NSI) is built upon this principle. Rather than simply analyzing symptoms from a cognitive perspective, NSI engages the **body-brain feedback loop**, working from the bottom up to influence top-down processes. This integrative approach leverages neuroplasticity through:

- **Somatic drills** that stimulate the vagus nerve and retrain brain-body pathways

- **Interoceptive awareness** to refine internal mapping of safety and emotional signals

- **Relational attunement** to restore healthy attachment and co-regulation

- **Consistent pattern disruption and reinforcement** to rewire habitual responses

As these inputs accumulate, they **repattern outputs**, resulting in new behaviors, emotional resilience, and enhanced capacity for self-regulation.

Science in Practice: The Mechanisms of Rewiring

Neuroplastic change requires:

- **Novelty**: A new stimulus or experience outside the existing survival pattern

- **Repetition**: Ongoing exposure to the new response or behavior

- **Safety**: A calm or co-regulated state that signals the brain it's safe to release the old pathway

- **Embodiment**: Full-body awareness and engagement that activate sensory-motor and emotional circuits

These elements work synergistically to **strengthen new neural connections** while gradually weakening the maladaptive ones. This is a biological process—not just a psychological one—and it is available to every person, regardless of age, trauma history, or diagnosis.

> "Neurons that fire together, wire together. But neurons that fire in safety, rewire for resilience."

Reclaiming Agency Through Neuroplasticity

Many people live with the belief that their reactions are fixed—that they are "just anxious," "always triggered," "prone to burnout," or "bad at relationships." But NSI teaches us to see these patterns for what they truly are: **learned survival responses** that can be **unlearned and replaced** with more supportive ones.

By consistently practicing body-based regulation, we build a new internal map—one rooted in choice, responsiveness, and empowerment. Over time, we go from reacting in survival mode to responding from a place of **embodied self-leadership**.

This is not about perfection. It is about **practice**. And with practice, the nervous system learns a new way of being in the world—grounded, present, and fully alive.

References
- **Doidge, N. (2007).** *The Brain That Changes Itself: Stories of personal triumph from the frontiers of brain science.* Penguin.

- **Kolb, B., & Whishaw, I. Q. (2009).** *Fundamentals of Human*

Neuropsychology (6th ed.). Worth Publishers.

- **Siegel, D. J. (2020).** *The Developing Mind: How relationships and the brain interact to shape who we are* (3rd ed.). Guilford Press.

- **Davidson, R. J., & Begley, S. (2012).** *The Emotional Life of Your Brain: How its unique patterns affect the way you think, feel, and live—and how you can change them.* Hudson Street Press.

The Daily Practice of Regulation

Regulation is not a destination—it is a discipline. Much like physical fitness, **nervous system health requires consistent, intentional practice** to build flexibility, resilience, and adaptability over time. One regulated moment may feel like a breakthrough, but it is the **cumulative repetition of self-regulation strategies** that creates long-term neural rewiring.

For those practicing **Neurosomatic Intelligence (NSI)**, nervous system regulation becomes a daily ritual. These routines are not generic; they are personalized and responsive to the individual's unique nervous system profile, trauma history, baseline arousal patterns, and environmental context.

Components of a Nervous System Hygiene Routine

NSI-based regulation tools target multiple sensory and neural pathways. These tools are designed to gently stimulate or calm the autonomic nervous system, particularly the **vagus nerve**, which plays a central role in shifting between survival states and restorative states.

Core Practices Include:

- **Orienting Practices**
  Ground the individual in the present moment by visually

and spatially scanning the environment.
Examples: Eye-tracking, mapping surroundings, "look and name" grounding
Validated by research on spatial attention and neural threat appraisal (Schauer & Elbert, 2010)

- **Breath Regulation**
Modulates heart rate variability (HRV) and parasympathetic tone.
Examples: Box breathing, extended exhale, humming, diaphragmatic breath
Lehrer & Gevirtz (2014) have shown HRV biofeedback improves vagal tone and anxiety regulation

- **Vagus Nerve Stimulation**
Directly activates the parasympathetic nervous system.
Examples: Singing, chanting, cold exposure, gargling, vocal toning
Tracey (2002) describes the vagus nerve's role in the inflammatory reflex and systemic calm

- **Interoceptive Drills**
Enhance awareness of internal body states and support emotional regulation.
Examples: Body scanning, heartbeat tracking, gut check-in
Craig (2002) emphasizes interoception as key to self-awareness and affective homeostasis

- **Movement Protocols**
Use proprioception and vestibular input to stabilize and integrate sensory data.
Examples: Gentle stretching, joint mobility, somatic shaking, slow spinal rolls
Ogden et al. (2006) support movement-based interventions in sensorimotor psychotherapy

- **Somatic Safety Cues**
  Anchor the body in feelings of safety and self-trust.
  Examples: Hand on heart, weighted blankets, rhythmic tapping, soothing touch
  Dana (2018) links safety cues to ventral vagal activation and social engagement system repair

These techniques function as **daily neural training**, helping individuals return to baseline more efficiently after stress and gradually expand their **Window of Tolerance**—a concept introduced by Dr. Dan Siegel (2020) to describe the optimal arousal range where a person can think, feel, and relate without becoming overwhelmed or shut down.

Building a Daily Regulation Practice

Like physical exercise, nervous system hygiene must be:

- **Consistent** – Regular use is more impactful than intensity

- **Personalized** – No one-size-fits-all; some systems need more activation, others more soothing

- **Responsive** – Adapted to your current state (e.g., hyperaroused vs. hypoaroused)

- **Compassionate** – Not a checklist, but a dialogue with your body

"Regulation is not about control. It's about **cooperation** with the body's innate wisdom."

Even 5–10 minutes of intentional somatic practice per day can create meaningful shifts in tone, mood, clarity, and relational capacity. Over time, these practices teach the nervous system that it is safe to down-regulate—and safe to stay present.

References

- Craig, A. D. (2002). How do you feel? Interoception: the sense of the physiological condition of the body. *Nature Reviews Neuroscience, 3*(8), 655–666.

- Dana, D. (2018). *The Polyvagal Theory in Therapy: Engaging the rhythm of regulation.* W. W. Norton & Company.

- Lehrer, P., & Gevirtz, R. (2014). Heart rate variability biofeedback: How and why does it work? *Frontiers in Psychology, 5,* 756.

- Ogden, P., Minton, K., & Pain, C. (2006). *Trauma and the Body: A Sensorimotor Approach to Psychotherapy.* W. W. Norton & Company.

- Schauer, M., & Elbert, T. (2010). Dissociation following traumatic stress: Etiology and treatment. *Journal of Psychology, 218*(2), 109–127.

- Siegel, D. J. (2020). *The Developing Mind: How relationships and the brain interact to shape who we are* (3rd ed.). Guilford Press.

- Tracey, K. J. (2002). The inflammatory reflex. *Nature, 420*(6917), 853–859.

Trauma, Chronic Stress, and Nervous System Fatigue

The human body is hardwired for survival. Whether a threat is real, imagined, or remembered, the nervous system responds in the same biologically programmed ways. It does not discriminate between a lion in the room and a painful memory that resurfaces in conversation—the **physiological response is**

activated either way.

When individuals are exposed to **chronic, cumulative, or overwhelming stressors**—such as adverse childhood experiences (ACEs), racial and systemic oppression, intimate partner violence, medical trauma, or poverty—the body's internal alarm system remains **on high alert**. Over time, this hyperactivation of the **hypothalamic-pituitary-adrenal (HPA) axis** leads to an overproduction and eventual dysregulation of cortisol, the body's primary stress hormone (McEwen, 1998; Sapolsky, 2004).

This condition, often referred to as **allostatic load** or **threat fatigue**, can result in a wide array of downstream symptoms:

- Heightened inflammation

- Sleep disturbances

- Impaired memory and concentration

- Digestive issues and hormone imbalance

- Emotional volatility or numbness

- Weakened immune function

- Increased vulnerability to autoimmune disorders, anxiety, and depression

The Nervous System Is Not Broken—It's Exhausted

In many clinical and educational settings, these symptoms are misinterpreted as **deficits**—a lack of motivation, discipline, or capacity. Clients and students are often labeled as resistant, avoidant, disinterested, or lazy.

From a **trauma-informed and Neurosomatic perspective**, however, these are not signs of dysfunction. They are evidence of a system that has been pushed beyond its threshold and has adapted by going into **shutdown, hypoarousal, or dissociation**—incredibly effective survival strategies for conserving energy and protecting the self when escape or resolution is not possible.

What looks like disinterest may actually be **dorsal vagal collapse.**
What appears to be laziness may be a **nervous system stuck in freeze.**
What is called defiance may be a **fight response to powerlessness.**

This paradigm shift—from pathology to **physiology**—reframes the narrative from shame to compassion. It allows both practitioners and individuals to stop asking, *"What's wrong with me?"* and instead ask, *"What has happened to my nervous system?"*

NSI and the Path Back to Capacity

Neurosomatic Intelligence provides a structured, embodied framework for helping individuals **rebuild capacity** after chronic stress and trauma. Instead of trying to "push through" dysregulation with mental effort, NSI uses somatic strategies to support **bottom-up re-regulation:**

- **Restoring interoceptive safety**, so the body no longer reads stillness or silence as dangerous

- **Gradual titration**, introducing activation and challenge in small, digestible doses

- **Building stress resilience**, not by avoiding stress, but by learning how to complete the stress cycle

- **Recalibrating the Window of Tolerance**, so the nervous

system can flex between arousal and rest without collapse

This is not about fixing a broken system—it's about helping a brilliant system recover from burnout. Trauma does not remove a person's capacity for resilience—it temporarily buries it beneath protective neural adaptations.

Biological Strategy, Not Character Defect

Understanding the nervous system's responses as intelligent—not pathological—is critical for trauma-informed practice. As Dr. Gabor Maté emphasizes, the survival adaptations we develop in the face of trauma are not flaws; they are **functional responses to unbearable conditions** (Maté, 2010).

By honoring these patterns as protective rather than punitive, NSI practitioners help clients:

- **Restore safety without shame**

- **Move from freeze to flow**

- **Reconnect to vitality, play, and presence**

Healing begins not with demanding more from a depleted system, but by helping that system **feel safe enough to rest, and strong enough to rise again.**

References
- **Maté, G. (2010).** *In the Realm of Hungry Ghosts: Close encounters with addiction.* North Atlantic Books.

- **McEwen, B. S. (1998).** Protective and damaging effects of stress mediators. *New England Journal of Medicine,* 338(3), 171–179.

- **Sapolsky, R. M. (2004).** *Why Zebras Don't Get Ulcers: The* *acclaimed guide to stress, stress-related diseases, and coping.* Holt Paperbacks.

- **Siegel, D. J. (2020).** *The Developing Mind: How relationships and the brain interact to shape who we are* (3rd ed.). Guilford Press.

- **van der Kolk, B. A. (2014).** *The Body Keeps the Score: Brain, mind, and body in the healing of trauma.* Viking.

CHAPTER 2

The Neurology of Beliefs, Identity, and Bias

Beliefs Begin in the Body

Beliefs are often thought of as intellectual constructs—ideas we adopt through reason or socialization. But in reality, beliefs are first formed as **felt experiences** in the body. Before we can articulate "I am safe" or "I am worthy," we must **feel** safe or worthy at the nervous system level. When the body consistently experiences fear, rejection, disempowerment, or chaos, the brain wires those somatic experiences into enduring beliefs about the self, the world, and others.

According to affective neuroscience and developmental psychology, beliefs about identity are built on **implicit memory systems**—those that operate beneath conscious awareness and are encoded somatically rather than semantically (Schore, 2003; Siegel, 2020). These early neural imprints shape the way we interpret social cues, form relationships, and view ourselves long before we develop language or logic.

> "The body tells the brain who we are before the mind can make meaning of it."

For example:

- A child repeatedly ignored may internalize the belief: *My voice doesn't matter.*

- A person exposed to cultural invalidation may somatically encode: *I must perform to be accepted.*

- A survivor of abuse may hold a deep, pre-verbal belief: *The world is not safe.*

These beliefs are not just thoughts—they are **neurobiological survival codes**.

The Implicit Brain and Identity Formation

Identity formation is a neurological process. In early development, the brain creates patterns of association based on experience and interoceptive feedback. These patterns form what psychologist Antonio Damasio calls the **"proto-self"— a nonverbal sense of self built from body-based experiences (Damasio, 1999)**.

When those early experiences are grounded in regulation, connection, and responsiveness, the identity that emerges tends to be adaptive, coherent, and resilient. But when those experiences are marked by abandonment, misattunement, or trauma, the developing nervous system adapts by encoding protective identities. These identities are not chosen; they are constructed by the body in service of safety.

Identity is not fixed; it is patterned.

These survival-based identities often persist long after the original threat has passed. For instance:

- A child who becomes the "fixer" in a chaotic home may become an adult who overfunctions in relationships.

- A young person raised in an environment where emotions were punished may adopt the identity of the "rational one", disconnected from their own feelings.

- A person who had to earn affection through perfectionism may identify as "the achiever," always striving but never arriving.

NSI helps individuals become aware of these identity patterns not as character flaws but as adaptive responses. Once brought into conscious awareness, they can be re-patterned.

The Neurobiology of Bias: How the Nervous System Sorts the World

Bias, like belief, is not merely a cognitive error—it is a **neurobiological adaptation**. The human brain is a pattern-seeking organ, constantly scanning the environment for cues of safety, threat, and familiarity. To conserve energy and reduce uncertainty, the nervous system engages in rapid classification of people, objects, and experiences based on prior exposure, internal states, and cultural conditioning (Barrett, 2017).

This rapid sorting process is governed in large part by the **limbic system**, particularly the **amygdala**, which plays a central role in social threat detection and emotional salience. Studies show that the amygdala activates more intensely in response to perceived "out-group" members, even without conscious awareness (Cikara & Van Bavel, 2014). This activation occurs milliseconds before the prefrontal cortex has a chance to assess or override the response, revealing that bias begins **below the level of conscious thought**—as a form of neuroception, or automatic risk assessment.

Bias as a State-Dependent Learning Process

When the nervous system is dysregulated—through trauma, chronic stress, or developmental adversity—its capacity to sort flexibly is impaired. Instead of discerning nuance, the brain defaults to protective generalizations. This state-dependent learning becomes encoded as implicit memory, forming the architecture of unconscious bias.

Factors that exacerbate implicit bias include:

- **Survival-based conditioning**: Individuals operating from a constant state of hypervigilance or freeze are more likely to perceive unfamiliarity as danger.

- **Cultural homogeneity**: Lack of exposure to diverse experiences and bodies increases the brain's reliance on stereotypes.

- **Systemic reinforcement**: Media, education, and institutional systems often propagate threat-based narratives about marginalized groups, embedding those narratives into the collective nervous system.

Thus, **bias is not simply an individual flaw—it is a byproduct of nervous system dysregulation within social environments shaped by inequality and fear** (Sue et al., 2007).

NSI and Bias Deconstruction

Neurosomatic Intelligence (NSI) offers a novel lens: **what if empathy begins with regulation?** When the nervous system is grounded and in a ventral vagal state (Porges, 2011), the brain's threat-detection system quiets, and the social engagement system activates. This allows for:

- Increased curiosity and openness to difference

- Greater cognitive flexibility

- Enhanced capacity for empathy and compassion

Regulation practices—such as breathwork, co-regulation, orienting, and somatic grounding—literally rewire the circuits involved in threat appraisal. Over time, these practices expand what the brain and body categorize as safe, familiar, and trustworthy.

Bias cannot be dismantled by logic alone. It must be met at the level where it lives: the nervous system.

Cultural Implications and Embodied Equity

In multicultural and therapeutic settings, it is critical to recognize that bias is not just implicit—it is embodied. For example:

- A clinician may unconsciously tighten their posture or shift tone when speaking to a client of a different race.

- An educator might misinterpret a student's body language as defiance when it is actually a trauma response.

- A leader may overlook or mistrust non-dominant ways of speaking, moving, or problem-solving due to somatic unfamiliarity.

When these patterns go unexamined, they perpetuate **somatic exclusion**—the experience of being perceived as unsafe, inappropriate, or "too much" simply by inhabiting one's body.

NSI-informed spaces intentionally address these dynamics through embodied equity practices, which include:

- Normalizing and honoring cultural variability in expression

- Training facilitators to track their own nervous system responses to difference

- Using body-based tools to shift from reaction to reflection

Bias work, then, becomes **healing work**—not just for the mind, but for the body and the collective field we share.

References

- **Barrett, L. F. (2017).** *How Emotions Are Made: The secret life of the brain.* Houghton Mifflin Harcourt.

- **Cikara, M., & Van Bavel, J. J. (2014).** The neuroscience of intergroup relations: An integrative review. *Perspectives on Psychological Science*, 9(3), 245–274.

- **Porges, S. W. (2011).** *The Polyvagal Theory: Neurophysiological foundations of emotions, attachment, communication, and self-regulation.* W. W. Norton & Company.

- **Sue, D. W., Capodilupo, C. M., Torino, G. C., Bucceri, J. M., Holder, A. M. B., Nadal, K. L., & Esquilin, M. (2007).** Racial microaggressions in everyday life: Implications for clinical practice. *American Psychologist*, 62(4), 271–286.

Trauma and the False Self: Survival-Based Identity Strategies

Identity is often mistaken for personality, but in trauma-informed somatic work, identity can also be understood as **a survival strategy**—a patterned set of behaviors, beliefs, and postures the nervous system adopts to stay safe in unsafe or unpredictable environments. When early experiences of disconnection, shame, abandonment, or threat occur, the developing nervous system adapts not to what is true, but to what is necessary.

This adaptive self is what trauma theorist Donald Winnicott termed the **"false self"**—a construct formed to meet the demands of others at the expense of one's authentic needs, desires, and sensations. In somatic terms, the false self is a composite of postural patterns, internalized roles, and emotional habits built to avoid rupture, rejection, or punishment.

Common Survival-Based Identities:

- **The Overachiever**: Driven by a hyperactivated nervous system and the belief that worth must be earned through performance, this identity overfunctions in order to avoid failure or rejection. Beneath the success lies a fear of not being enough.

- **The Caretaker**: This identity prioritizes others' needs while suppressing their own, often rooted in fawn responses and early enmeshment. Their nervous system equates self-sacrifice with safety and belonging.

- **The Invisible One**: This dissociative identity avoids conflict and scrutiny by minimizing presence—physically, emotionally, or energetically. Their system learned that visibility led to harm or neglect.

- **The Chameleon**: Highly attuned to the environment, this identity shape-shifts to meet perceived expectations, often losing their sense of internal orientation in the process.

These identities are not flaws or character defects—they are **intelligent neural adaptations** shaped by experience. From a Neurosomatic Intelligence (NSI) perspective, these strategies are not to be pathologized but understood with reverence and compassion. They were the body's way of surviving in a world that felt unsafe.

The Body Builds the Identity Before the Mind Does

Survival identities are not solely cognitive. They are **somatic**, encoded in muscle tone, posture, breath pattern, voice modulation, and internalized interoceptive cues. For instance:

- The overachiever may hold constant muscular tension in the jaw, neck, or shoulders—embodying hypervigilance.

- The caretaker may feel numb or disconnected from their own gut instincts, having been conditioned to ignore their needs.

- The invisible one may present with shallow breathing, collapsed posture, or low vocal tone, signaling dorsal vagal dominance.

This is why NSI prioritizes regulation before mindset change. **You cannot cognitively override an identity that is neurologically linked to your safety.** Change must begin with restoring physiological safety so that the system can release protective behaviors that are no longer necessary.

Reclaiming the Authentic Self

The goal of NSI is not to eradicate the false self, but to **create the internal safety required for the authentic self to emerge**—not just conceptually, but biologically. This process unfolds in stages:

1. **We Regulate First**
   Through breath, grounding, co-regulation, and somatic titration, we calm the body's protective reflexes and shift out of chronic threat response.

2. **We Rewire Second**
   Once regulation is established, the nervous system becomes receptive to new patterns. We introduce somatic practices, relationship templates, and interoceptive awareness that support authenticity.

3. **We Reimagine Third**
   Only after safety and flexibility are restored can we consciously explore new ways of being—ways that are congruent with our values, desires, and embodied truth.

This transformation is not about "fixing" who we were. It's

about liberating the parts of us that never got to be. NSI invites us to stop asking, "What's wrong with me?" and start asking, "What has my nervous system had to do to protect me—and what does it need now to let me live freely?"

> "The false self is not a lie. It's a love letter written in fear—waiting to be rewritten in safety."

Repatterning Beliefs Through Neurosomatic Tools

Belief systems are not solely formed through conscious thought—they are **encoded somatically** through repeated experience, emotional state, and nervous system activation. While traditional approaches to belief change emphasize mindset shifts, affirmations, or cognitive reframing, neuroscience shows that beliefs are state-dependent. This means that the **body's physiological condition directly influences what feels true.**

In states of dysregulation—whether hyperarousal (anxiety, overdrive) or hypoarousal (shutdown, numbness)—the brain filters information through a survival lens. In these states, affirmations like *"I am worthy"* or *"I am safe"* may feel alien or even triggering. Not because they're false, but because the nervous system is **not regulated enough to receive them**.

Neurosomatic Intelligence (NSI) provides a bottom-up, body-first approach to belief transformation. It begins with **changing the physiological state**, then introduces new beliefs while the system is grounded, coherent, and safe. This process ensures that beliefs are not just recited—they are **felt, integrated, and embodied**.

The NSI Method: A Stepwise Somatic Approach

1. Regulate: Create State Safety First

Start by shifting the nervous system from a protective state to one of openness and safety. This can be done through:

- **Breathwork** (e.g., extended exhale, box breathing)
- **Vagus nerve stimulation** (e.g., gargling, humming, cold exposure)
- **Orienting practices** (e.g., scanning the room, naming objects aloud)
- **Grounding exercises** (e.g., feeling feet on the floor, pressing palms together)

These tools quiet the limbic system and activate the ventral vagal circuit, restoring access to presence, curiosity, and integration.

2. Resource: Anchor in Internal Cues of Safety

Once regulation is established, shift awareness inward to identify **felt sensations of safety** or neutrality. This may include:

- Steady heartbeat
- Warmth in the chest
- Relaxed jaw or shoulders
- Grounded contact with the floor or seat
- A memory or image that evokes comfort

These sensations become **somatic anchors**, allowing the nervous system to recognize that it is no longer in danger.

3. Rewire: Introduce the New Belief in Regulation

Now introduce the desired belief—**but only while the body is regulated**. For example:

- While feeling grounded: "I am allowed to take up space."

- While breathing calmly: "It's safe to let others in."

- While placing a hand on the heart: "My needs matter."

The pairing of new belief with **internal safety cues** is what begins the rewiring process. The nervous system learns, through experience, that these new truths are not only possible—they are survivable.

4. Reinforce: Practice with Consistency and Compassion

Neural plasticity is built through **repetition and emotion**. Practicing this belief-state pairing daily strengthens the new neural pathway and diminishes the old threat response. Reinforcement can include:

- Somatic journaling or voice affirmations during breathwork

- Embodied role play in a coaching or therapeutic space

- Movement or gestures that symbolize the new identity

- Returning to somatic anchors when challenged or triggered

This consistent engagement reshapes the body-brain belief loop—not through force, but through gentle, relational self-practice.

Why This Works: The Science of Somatic Belief Change

This method is grounded in core principles of **interoception,** neuroplasticity, and state-dependent memory:

- **Interoception** (Craig, 2002): Awareness of internal bodily states enhances emotional and cognitive integration.

- **Neuroplasticity** (Doidge, 2007): The brain can form new connections when experiences are repeated with attention and safety.

- **State-Dependent Learning** (Siegel, 2020): What the nervous system learns in a regulated state is fundamentally different than what it absorbs under stress.

By weaving new beliefs into moments of embodied safety, individuals don't just think differently—they **feel differently**, behave differently, and lead differently. The shift becomes sustainable because it is rooted in **physiological coherence**, not willpower.

"You cannot think your way into a new identity—you must feel your way into a new truth."

Somatic Practice: The "I Am" Rewire

The statements we attach to *"I am"* are not just affirmations—they are **identity scripts**. These scripts are often formed during early developmental windows, when the nervous system is highly impressionable and reliant on external feedback for internal regulation. For individuals with trauma, neglect, or chronic stress, the *"I am"* narrative may have been unconsciously shaped by pain:

- *"I am not enough."*

- *"I am too much."*

- *"I am a burden."*

Changing these narratives cannot occur through language alone. It requires pairing **new identity statements** with regulated somatic states that allow the body to **experience** the new truth as safe, real, and livable.

The **"I Am" Rewire** is a core Neurosomatic Intelligence (NSI) practice designed to shift deeply held identity patterns by engaging both the **cognitive and physiological systems**. It is not a performance—it is a **relational experience between the self and the nervous system**.

Step-by-Step: The "I Am" Rewire Protocol

Step 1: Choose a Core Identity Statement

Select one **"I am"** phrase that resonates with your healing intention or desired identity. Keep it simple, present-tense, and emotionally potent:

- *"I am safe."*
- *"I am allowed to rest."*
- *"I am worthy of love."*
- *"I am powerful."*
- *"I am enough."*

Choose only **one** phrase at a time—this helps prevent overwhelm and allows deeper integration.

Step 2: Regulate the Nervous System

Begin by creating a somatic state of safety. Choose one regulating practice to downshift arousal and activate the ventral vagal system:

- **Humming**: Activates the vagus nerve and soothes the brainstem

- **Heart Coherence Breathing**: Inhale for 5 seconds, exhale for 5 seconds while focusing on the heart

- **Self-holding**: Place one hand on the chest and one on the belly

- **Orienting**: Slowly look around the room, noticing colors, textures, and light

Spend at least 2–3 minutes in this regulation phase to ensure the nervous system is open and receptive.

Step 3: Speak the Belief in Embodied Safety

Gently speak your chosen *"I am"* statement aloud. As you speak, **tune in** to your breath, posture, and tone of voice. Ask yourself:

- *Does this feel true in my body?*

- *Where do I feel openness or resistance?*

- *What sensations arise when I say this?*

If resistance arises, that's normal. Simply **stay regulated** and soften. You may place a hand over your heart or take a deep breath as you repeat the phrase:

> *"I am enough." (exhale)*
> *"I am enough." (with hand on chest)*
> *"I am enough." (standing tall, shoulders relaxed)*

These subtle shifts make the new belief **experiential**, not just conceptual.

Step 4: Repeat with Sensory Anchoring

Repeat the practice daily, ideally at the same time and in the same place. To deepen the somatic imprint, include:

- **Postural alignment**: Stand or sit with an empowered stance (feet grounded, spine tall)

- **Vocal tone**: Use a steady, grounded voice

- **Eye contact**: Speak into a mirror to integrate visual and verbal input

- **Sensory layering**: Light a calming candle, wear a comforting texture, or play gentle background music

These sensory anchors reinforce the **multi-channel integration** of the new identity.

Why It Works

This practice is rooted in the science of:

- **State-dependent encoding** (Siegel, 2020): New beliefs are more easily retained when introduced during a regulated state.

- **Neuroplasticity** (Doidge, 2007): Repetition in safety rewires belief pathways in the brain.

- **Embodiment theory** (Damasio, 1999): Identity is not just formed in the mind—it is formed in the body.

Over time, the nervous system begins to associate your "*I am*" statement with safety, congruence, and agency. The belief becomes **not just something you say—but something you know**.

Your words shape your nervous system. Your body remembers the tone, the rhythm, and the feeling of truth. Speak your future into your fascia—your cells are listening.

Identity Is a Nervous System Story

Identity is not a fixed destination—it is a **living, breathing process** constantly shaped by the nervous system's interpretation of safety, connection, and experience. From birth onward, the body scans its environment and encodes responses not just to events, but to the **felt sense of those events**. These felt experiences form the blueprint of who we believe we are.

What we call *"self"* is in fact an emergent pattern of **neurological conditioning**—a dynamic blend of:

- Interoceptive awareness (how we sense the internal state of the body)

- Social and relational feedback (how others respond to us)

- Nervous system states (regulated or dysregulated)

- Implicit memory (what the body remembers, even if the mind does not)

When these experiences are grounded in safety, attunement, and connection, the nervous system builds a flexible, adaptive identity. But when shaped by trauma, abandonment, systemic harm, or chronic dysregulation, identity becomes **narrow, reactive, and protective**. We form roles to survive: the achiever, the pleaser, the ghost, the rock. These are not character flaws—they are **embodied adaptations.**

Neuroscience confirms that identity is not hardwired—it is **patterned**. The brain's **default mode network (DMN)**, which is involved in self-referential thinking and autobiographical memory, is heavily influenced by emotional salience and trauma history (Raichle et al., 2001). If early environments were unsafe or unpredictable, the DMN can loop stories of unworthiness, fear, or hypervigilance without conscious awareness.

The amygdala scans for social threat, encoding relational pain as danger. The hippocampus may fragment or silence memory under extreme stress. The prefrontal cortex, responsible for self-reflection and regulation, is less active during chronic dysregulation.

In other words: **we don't just think our identity—we feel it. We somatize it. We live it in the tissues, breath patterns, and postural habits of our everyday existence.**

Reclaiming the Narrative Through NSI

Neurosomatic Intelligence reframes identity as a **story the nervous system has been telling to protect us**—a story that can be rewritten when safety, awareness, and embodied presence are restored.

> You are not broken. You adapted.
> Your beliefs are not you. They are patterns.
> Safety is the soil where new identities can grow.

This approach does not seek to fix or erase survival-based identities. It seeks to **befriend them**—to meet them with reverence and compassion, to understand why they arose, and to slowly make room for something deeper, truer, and more whole to emerge.

Through consistent regulation, body-based practices, and intentional repetition, we teach the nervous system a new baseline:

- That rest is not dangerous

- That presence is not punishment

- That softness does not mean weakness

- That you can be seen and still be safe

From this place, identity becomes **an invitation**—not a prison.

Nervous System State	Typical Emotional State	Common Identity Expression	Adaptive Function
Ventral Vagal (Regulated)	Calm, Connected, Empowered	Authentic, Self, Leader, Creative	Engagement, Presence, Growth
Sympathetic (Fight/Flight)	Anxious, Angry, Reactive	Fixer, Performer, Protector	Protection, Hypervigilance, Survival
Dorsal Vagal (Freeze/Shutdown)	Numb, Hopeless, Disconeccted	Invisible One, Outsider, Ghost	Conservation, Withdrawal, Survival

Figure 2. Nervous System States and Identity Patterns

This chart illustrates how different states of nervous system activation correspond to emotional tendencies, identity expressions, and adaptive survival functions.

Embodied Inquiry for Identity Reclamation

As you consider your own story, ask not just:

- *Who am I?*
  But also:

- *What state am I in when I ask that question?*

- *Does my body feel safe to explore new possibilities?*

- *Am I telling the story of my life from survival... or from sovereignty?*

These questions engage the nervous system in the identity process. They acknowledge that before you can *become* who you are meant to be, you must first **feel safe enough to be**.

Identity is not a diagnosis—it is a dance. A choreography between the body, the brain, the breath, and the stories we carry.

In NSI, we don't force change. We create the **conditions** for emergence. We regulate first, rewire second, and reimagine third. Through this process, the story of self transforms from one of endurance to one of embodiment.

You are not your trauma.
You are not the role you played to survive.
You are the author now.

References

- **Cikara, M., & Van Bavel, J. J. (2014).** The neuroscience of intergroup relations: An integrative review. *Perspectives on Psychological Science*, 9(3), 245–274.

- **Damasio, A. R. (1999).** *The Feeling of What Happens: Body and emotion in the making of consciousness.* Harcourt Brace.

- **Schore, A. N. (2003).** *Affect Dysregulation and Disorders of the Self.* W. W. Norton & Company.

- **Siegel, D. J. (2020).** *The Developing Mind: How relationships and the brain interact to shape who we are* (3rd ed.). Guilford Press.

CHAPTER 3
Emotional Regulation and Somatic Expression

Emotions as Energetic and Neurological States

Emotions are not just psychological experiences—they are full-body neurological events. Every emotion we feel is accompanied by a cascade of changes in the brain, body, and nervous system. From increased heart rate and muscle tension to shifts in hormone levels and vagal tone, emotions are physical responses to internal or external stimuli.

In Neurosomatic Intelligence (NSI), we understand emotions as **adaptive information loops** designed to signal the nervous system about relational, environmental, or internal conditions. These signals are not meant to be suppressed or ignored; they are meant to be **felt, understood, and moved**. When emotional energy is interrupted, denied, or shamed, it becomes stored as somatic residue, creating patterns of dysregulation and chronic stress.

> "Emotion is energy in motion. To regulate it, we must first allow it to move."

The Role of the Nervous System in Emotional Regulation

Emotional regulation is the nervous system's ability to respond to stimuli without becoming overwhelmed or shut down. It is a function of both **autonomic balance**—the dynamic interplay between sympathetic activation (mobilization) and parasympathetic restoration (rest and digest)—and **cortical integration**, especially involving the **prefrontal cortex**, which governs executive function, impulse control, and emotional modulation.

When the nervous system is well-regulated, emotional responses are fluid, proportionate, and context-sensitive. The body can experience emotions fully without being hijacked by them. However, when the nervous system is dysregulated due to trauma, chronic stress, or unresolved emotional patterns, regulation breaks down and emotional responses become extreme, unpredictable, or entirely inaccessible:

- **Hyperaroused states** may present as anxiety, panic, rage, irritability, hypervigilance, or compulsive reactivity. These are signs that the system is stuck in a chronic fight-or-flight loop.

- **Hypoaroused states** may present as numbness, emotional blunting, depression, fatigue, brain fog, or shutdown. These reflect dominance of the dorsal vagal system—a protective freeze response.

In both cases, the emotional system is not malfunctioning—it is **overprotecting**. The body is trying to manage perceived threat, even when none is present in the current moment.

The NSI approach to regulation does not pathologize these states. Instead, it views them as **survival strategies**—brilliant biological adaptations the body has adopted in response to unsafe or overwhelming experiences. This lens removes the shame and blame from emotional dysregulation and replaces it with compassion, understanding, and physiological re-education.

By restoring regulation through somatic tools like breathwork, interoceptive awareness, movement, and co-regulation, the system regains its ability to:

- Experience emotions fully without becoming overwhelmed

- Shift between emotional states with flexibility
- Respond rather than react
- Access empathy, presence, and clear decision-making

Over time, this process increases the nervous system's **window of tolerance** and builds the internal safety required for emotional expression and integration.

Somatic Expression: Completing the Emotional Loop

Every emotion has a **biological completion cycle** that involves sensing, identifying, expressing, and releasing the felt experience. In many Western contexts, individuals are taught to inhibit emotional expression in favor of composure, performance, or safety. This conditioning often begins early in life, where emotional suppression is rewarded as a sign of maturity or strength, while vulnerability is viewed as weakness or instability.

The reality is that emotional suppression is not cultural resilience—it is biological fragmentation. And this fragmentation disproportionately affects individuals across cultural, racial, and gendered lines. In many BIPOC communities, for instance, emotional stoicism has been necessary for survival in environments that criminalize or pathologize emotional expression. Black, Indigenous, and Latinx children are often taught to "be strong," "stay quiet," or "never show them how you feel"—adaptive strategies born from systemic oppression and collective trauma. While culturally protective, these patterns can create long-term somatic consequences when left unprocessed.

NSI emphasizes that **healthy somatic expression** is not indulgent—it is essential. It is how the nervous system metabolizes emotional energy and completes unresolved biological loops. Reclaiming the right to express is not just a nervous system intervention—it is an act of healing justice.

Examples of somatic expression practices include:

- Shaking, trembling, or bouncing to release sympathetic charge
- Sounding (sighing, moaning, vocalizing) to stimulate the vagus nerve
- Movement sequences that mimic the body's natural responses (e.g., fists for anger, curling for fear)
- Embodied role-play or dramatic enactment in a regulated state

These practices must be guided by safety and titration. The goal is not to reenact trauma, but to allow the nervous system to safely complete what it could not at the time of the original experience. Creating culturally responsive, consent-based environments for these practices allows people to reconnect with their emotional truth without fear of judgment, punishment, or retraumatization.

The Science Behind Somatic Expression

Research in affective neuroscience, trauma therapy, and sensorimotor psychotherapy supports the efficacy of somatic expression in emotional processing. Somatic expression serves as the bridge between autonomic arousal and emotional integration, transforming dysregulated states into embodied coherence through movement, sound, gesture, and breath.

- **Van der Kolk (2014)** describes how trauma is stored in subcortical regions of the brain and body, often inaccessible through language alone. He emphasizes the importance of somatic and sensory processing in trauma recovery, noting that movement and body awareness reengage neural circuits responsible for regulation and self-awareness.

- **Levine (1997)** introduces the concept of "completing the defensive orienting response," which refers to the body's instinctive attempts to fight, flee, or freeze when threatened. When these impulses are interrupted—as they often are in trauma—the body remains stuck in an incomplete stress response. Somatic expression helps discharge that trapped energy and restore homeostasis.

- **Porges (2011)** outlines how vocalization, facial expressivity, and rhythmic movement are essential features of the social engagement system governed by the ventral vagus nerve. Stimulating this system through embodied expression increases vagal tone and creates a sense of interpersonal safety and connection.

- **Ogden et al. (2006)** detail how trauma disrupts the body's innate motor sequences and defensive gestures. These incomplete movements become frozen in the sensorimotor system, contributing to symptoms such as tension, hyperarousal, or numbness. Through structured somatic practices, these motor patterns can be re-integrated, allowing the individual to complete their emotional responses in a safe and embodied way.

Recent studies also demonstrate that expressive movement practices (e.g., dance therapy, somatic experiencing, and trauma-informed yoga) significantly reduce cortisol levels, improve emotion regulation, and enhance interoceptive awareness (Price & Hooven, 2018; Van de Kamp et al., 2019).

These findings affirm what embodied traditions have long known: the body is not simply the container of emotion—it is the primary processor. To heal emotional wounds, we must restore the body's role as both messenger and mover.

Regulating Through Expression: A Somatic Sequence

Emotional regulation is not just about suppression or redirection—it's about allowing the nervous system to **complete**

the loop of an emotional experience while staying grounded in safety. This somatic sequence is a step-by-step method to support real-time emotional processing, integration, and nervous system coherence.

Step 1: Notice the Signal

Pause and attune to your body. Identify a physiological cue that an emotion is present. This could include a tight chest, shallow breath, clenched jaw, racing thoughts, gut tension, or fidgeting. Bringing mindful awareness to these somatic signals is the first act of regulation.

Step 2: Name the State

Without judgment, name the emotional state you are experiencing. Labeling the emotion (e.g., anger, grief, joy, fear, shame) reduces amygdala activation and reengages the prefrontal cortex—creating space between sensation and reaction. If you're unsure of the emotion, stay curious and describe the sensation instead.

Step 3: Choose a Practice

Select a somatic practice that corresponds to the energy of the emotion. For instance:

- Anger may benefit from punching a pillow, stomping, or breath of fire.
- Grief may call for rocking, curling, humming, or slow deep breathing.
- Fear may respond to orienting practices, grounding, or shaking.
- Joy may be amplified through movement, dancing, or laughter.

The key is to choose a practice that is **congruent** with the emotion's natural rhythm.

Step 4: Regulate in Real Time

While engaging in the chosen practice, add a layer of regulation: grounding through the feet, placing a hand on the chest or belly, extending the exhale, or using rhythmic breath. These additions help anchor the expression in safety so that the nervous system can complete the cycle without tipping into overwhelm.

Step 5: Reflect and Reorient

After the expression has moved through, pause to observe your internal state. Has your breath changed? Has the tension shifted? Do you feel more present, clearer, or connected? This reflection helps track progress, deepen self-trust, and reinforce regulation as a felt experience—not just a concept.

This somatic sequence can be used preventatively or responsively. Practiced daily, it builds emotional literacy, resilience, and a more compassionate relationship with your nervous system. Over time, it teaches the body that it is **safe to feel**—and that all emotions can be expressed without danger or collapse.

Your Body Speaks in Feeling

Emotions are not problems to solve—they are **messages from the nervous system**, asking us to listen, feel, and respond. Each emotion carries with it an energetic signature and a neurophysiological message designed to guide us toward balance, insight, or action. When we allow these messages to be expressed through the body—without shame, suppression, or judgment—we restore internal coherence and strengthen our connection to self and others.

In a world that often prioritizes productivity over presence and logic over embodiment, relearning how to feel is a radical act. Many of us have been conditioned to distrust our emotional impulses, to fear the depth of our sadness, or to suppress our rage. Over time, this disconnection from emotion translates into disconnection from the body, from self-worth, and from our internal compass.

NSI teaches us that emotional intelligence is not just a cognitive skill. It is a **somatic language**, spoken through breath, posture, movement, and sensation. Fluency in this language allows us to become interpreters of our own nervous system—and to respond with curiosity, compassion, and intentionality.

To reclaim emotional expression is to reclaim power, dignity, and embodiment. To feel is not a liability—it is a pathway to healing. When we embrace the full spectrum of our emotions as allies instead of adversaries, we begin to live from a place of grounded aliveness. We step into our capacity to lead, to connect, and to heal—not just ourselves, but the communities we serve.

You are not too much. Your feelings are not too loud. Your body is speaking—and it deserves to be heard.

References

- **Levine, P. A. (1997).** *Waking the Tiger: Healing trauma.* North Atlantic Books.

- **Ogden, P., Minton, K., & Pain, C. (2006).** *Trauma and the Body: A sensorimotor approach to psychotherapy.* W. W. Norton & Company.

- **Porges, S. W. (2011).** *The Polyvagal Theory: Neurophysiological foundations of emotions, attachment, communication, and self-regulation.* W. W. Norton & Company.

- **van der Kolk, B. A. (2014).** *The Body Keeps the Score: Brain, mind, and body in the healing of trauma.* Viking.

SECTION II: PATTERNS OF PROTECTION AND DYSREGULATION

CHAPTER 4

Freeze, Dissociation, and Survival-Based Shutdown

When the Body Protects by Disappearing

Before we could speak, before we could explain, our bodies learned how to survive. For some of us, survival meant fighting back or fleeing the scene. But for many others—especially in situations where resistance or escape were impossible—**the body chose to disappear**.

The freeze, flop, and fawn responses are not character flaws. They are intelligent, physiological survival strategies—rooted in our autonomic nervous system. These states are often misunderstood, overlooked, or mislabeled as laziness, disinterest, or weakness. In reality, they are **neurobiological shields** forged in overwhelming environments.

Neurosomatic Intelligence (NSI) helps us understand these states not as pathologies to fix, but as patterns to honor and transform. This chapter will explore how dissociation, immobilization, and people-pleasing function as *adaptive armor*, and how we can begin to safely return to our bodies, reclaim presence, and rewire connection.

Understanding Freeze and Dissociation

In Polyvagal Theory (Porges, 2011), the **dorsal vagal pathway** governs the freeze and shutdown response. When neither fight nor flight is possible, the body opts for immobilization. This can feel like numbness, exhaustion, blankness, or disconnection from time and space.

This response originates in the most ancient part of the

vagus nerve and is shared with many species as a last-resort survival mechanism. When escape is impossible, playing dead becomes the only option.

In childhood trauma or chronically unsafe environments, this dissociative adaptation becomes a baseline. The body learns: *It is safer not to feel.* In these states, the body and mind disconnect—often leading to a fragmented sense of self and difficulty accessing felt experience.

Signs of freeze/dissociation include:

- Spacing out or losing time
- Chronic fatigue or fogginess
- Difficulty sensing internal states (low interoception)
- "Going blank" during conflict or intimacy
- Avoidance of intense emotional or physical sensation

Neuroscientific studies show that dissociation correlates with reduced activation in areas such as the insula and anterior cingulate cortex—regions responsible for interoception and self-awareness (Lanius et al., 2010).

Rather than shame these patterns, NSI practitioners invite **somatic curiosity**. Dissociation is not disobedience—it is protection. It's not a problem to fix, but a signal to decode. With enough safety, we can gently invite the body back into connection.

This is a slow process. We don't "force" presence—we create the conditions for it to arise.

Fawn and Flop: When Connection Becomes Compliance

The **fawn response** is often missed in traditional trauma models. It refers to the reflexive strategy of appeasing others to avoid conflict, abandonment, or violence. It's common in individuals who grew up in unpredictable homes, experienced emotionally immature caregivers, or navigated high-demand environments where survival depended on pleasing others.

Fawning might look like:

- Over-apologizing or overexplaining
- Losing personal preferences or boundaries
- Hyper-vigilance around others' emotions
- Saying "yes" when your body screams "no"
- Difficulty asserting needs, desires, or limits
- Feeling responsible for others' emotional states

While it may appear as kindness or helpfulness on the surface, fawning is rooted in fear. It's the body's way of saying, *If I stay agreeable, I might stay safe.*

The **flop response**, often overlooked, refers to sudden physical or emotional collapse in the face of overwhelm. This may manifest as:

- Slumping posture or sudden fatigue
- Inability to speak, act, or think clearly
- Emotional flatlining or internal "shutdown"
- Withdrawing completely during stress or conflict

Flop can follow a sympathetic spike that's too intense for the system to handle—like the nervous system pulling the emergency brake. It is not weakness. It is wisdom born of survival.

Both fawn and flop represent adaptations of the autonomic nervous system to environments where assertiveness, resistance, or even presence felt dangerous. These patterns often persist into adulthood, particularly in relationships, leadership, or high-stress situations.

Through NSI, we learn to recognize these patterns not as faults, but as **somatic communication**. They tell us about the body's story—where safety was once compromised, and how it tried to protect us. And most importantly, they offer us a place to begin.

By cultivating safety, tracking sensation, and practicing small acts of self-assertion and embodiment, we begin to reclaim our boundaries, our preferences, and our power.

The goal is not to stop fawning or flopping through force or shame. The goal is to widen the Window of Tolerance so these patterns are no longer the only options available.

Trauma's Imprint on the Nervous System

Trauma is not defined by the external event—it is the internal experience of overwhelm that exceeds our capacity to process and integrate. It's the body's **incomplete survival response**, frozen in time.

When we experience threat without the ability to fight, flee, or be comforted afterward, our autonomic nervous system initiates protective responses—fight, flight, freeze, fawn, or flop—that often cannot complete. That incomplete energy doesn't just disappear; it gets **stored in the body's tissues, neural pathways, and somatic memory**.

Over time, this survival-based imprint creates deep shifts in:

- **Relational patterns**: Hypervigilance, people-pleasing, or emotional withdrawal in relationships become default ways to seek safety.

- **Self-identity**: Beliefs like *"I am too much," "I am not safe,"* or *"My needs don't matter"* take root in the nervous system, not just the mind.

- **Physiological health**: Chronic dysregulation can manifest as pain syndromes, digestive issues, adrenal fatigue, autoimmune conditions, or sleep disturbances.

Neuroimaging studies have shown that trauma changes the structure and function of key brain regions such as the **amygdala** (heightened fear detection), **hippocampus** (impaired memory consolidation), and **prefrontal cortex** (reduced executive functioning and emotional regulation) (McEwen, 1998; Bremner, 2006). Additionally, **fascia and muscle tissue** can hold somatic tension for decades, manifesting as unexplained tightness or chronic pain (Van der Kolk, 2014; Scaer, 2005).

In NSI, we don't just address symptoms. We **trace the survival pattern back to its physiological root**. Through bottom-up somatic practices, we help the body do what it couldn't do then: **complete the response, discharge the stored energy, and return to regulation**.

This is not just about healing the past—it's about **reshaping the present**.

The invitation is not to relive the trauma, but to **relate differently to the body's story**. By creating safe, sensory-based experiences of presence, we give the nervous system what it needed back then: choice, control, and connection.

This is where true transformation begins—not by thinking our way to healing, but by feeling our way home.

Coming Back Into the Body: NSI Practices for Reconnection

Reclaiming embodiment is not a linear journey—it is a sacred process of *re-entering the body one breath, one sensation, one choice at a time*. For individuals who have experienced chronic trauma, dissociation, or emotional overwhelm, the body can feel more like a battleground than a home.

Neurosomatic Intelligence (NSI) offers a gentle path back.

The goal is not to force presence but to *invite* it through safety, curiosity, and micro-experiences of regulation. We begin with what's tolerable. We listen for what's available. We build trust with the body in the language it speaks: sensation, rhythm, and safety.

Core NSI Practices for Reconnection

- **Interoceptive Tracking**: Trauma often severs our connection to internal cues. NSI trains individuals to **notice subtle bodily signals**—the warmth of hands, the pulse behind the eyes, the rise of breath in the belly. This restores interoception, the foundational awareness that reconnects mind and body.

- **Orienting to the Present**: Trauma roots us in the past; embodiment anchors us in the *now*. Orienting is the practice of using the **five senses to scan the environment** and signal to the brainstem that "here is not there." Gaze around the room, name five colors, feel your feet on the floor—this shifts the nervous system out of threat response and into present-moment awareness.

- **Micro-Movements**: When full-body expression feels too intense, we start small. **Gentle swaying, rocking, toe-wiggling, shoulder rolls, or tapping** the thighs offer non-threatening ways to reintroduce movement and sensation. These movements activate proprioceptive and vestibular systems, supporting safety and embodiment without overwhelm.

- **Vocalization and Sound**: Humming, sighing, or toning activate the **ventral vagal nerve**, sending a calming signal from the body to the brain. These vibrations resonate through the chest and throat, helping release tension and restore felt presence.

- **Co-Regulation Practices**: Healing in isolation is limited. Co-regulation invites **connection with a regulated other**

—a therapist, partner, friend, or group member who can offer safety through tone of voice, facial expression, and calm presence. Practices include:

- Mirrored breath
- Rhythmic rocking together
- Gentle touch with consent
- Shared grounding rituals

Cultural Sensitivity and Embodied Safety

Many BIPOC, LGBTQ+, and marginalized communities experience cultural and intergenerational trauma that make embodiment uniquely complex. For some, "coming back into the body" also means coming back into a body that has been objectified, policed, or excluded.

In these contexts, **reconnection must be culturally informed**. This might include:

- Using **ancestral practices** such as drumming, chanting, or dance as forms of somatic restoration.
- Grounding in **ritual, prayer, or spiritual adornment** to signal safety and belonging.
- Incorporating community-based co-regulation—family, elders, or collective healing circles.

Embodiment is not one-size-fits-all. NSI invites each person to reclaim their body in ways that feel culturally congruent, spiritually safe, and emotionally empowering.

The Nervous System Learns Through Repetition

These practices must be **repeated, not perfected**. The nervous system learns through gentle exposure, not force. Each time you choose to feel, to notice, to move—**you're rewriting your neural map of safety**.

With consistency, the body begins to believe:

I am not in danger. I can be here now. I belong in my body.

And from that place, deeper healing becomes possible.

The Promise of Reclamation

Dissociation and immobilization are not failures of will or signs of dysfunction. They are evidence of a nervous system that adapted wisely to circumstances beyond its capacity.

NSI offers a pathway toward reintegration by honoring the biology of protection and guiding individuals toward physiological and psychological safety.

The act of reclamation is not a return to a former self, but the emergence of a truer one—one that holds both pain and power, both history and hope.

In the subsequent chapters, we will examine additional protective strategies, such as anxiety, hypervigilance, anger, and reactivity. Each will be explored through the lens of somatic intelligence, offering not only insight but actionable tools for transformation.

Healing is not a correction. It is a reclamation of agency, presence, and wholeness.

CHAPTER 5

Anxiety and Overwhelm

When the Mind Won't Stop and the Body Won't Settle

Anxiety is often misunderstood as a purely cognitive issue—a restless mind caught in loops of overthinking, obsessive worry, and future-focused fear. Conventional approaches tend to target anxious thought patterns with logic or reframing. However, from a neuroscience and somatic perspective, anxiety is not just in the mind—it is in the body. It is a **nervous system state** rooted in dysregulation, hypervigilance, and unresolved survival energy.

When the body perceives threat—real or imagined—the autonomic nervous system mobilizes to protect us. The sympathetic branch activates, heart rate increases, breath shortens, and muscles tense in preparation for fight or flight. But in chronic stress, trauma, or environments where resolution was never achieved, this mobilization becomes maladaptive. The nervous system remains "on" even in moments of safety.

Neurosomatic Intelligence (NSI) reframes anxiety as more than a symptom. It is a **signal**—a call from the body for regulation, safety, and repair. When we begin to listen to anxiety through a somatic lens, we discover that beneath the panic is not weakness, but wisdom. The body is attempting to protect us with the tools it has, even if those tools are outdated survival responses.

This chapter explores the **neurobiology of chronic stress**, the **science of interoception**, and practical **NSI tools** for calming the system through breath, sensory awareness, and nervous system attunement. We will not only learn how to manage anxiety, but how to transform it—into clarity, containment, and embodied resilience.

The Neurobiology of Chronic Stress and Hypervigilance

When the nervous system is exposed to repeated or unpredictable stress, the **hypothalamic-pituitary-adrenal (HPA) axis** becomes overactive. Cortisol and adrenaline levels remain elevated, impairing the body's ability to return to baseline. This is not a psychological weakness—it is a **biological loop** of survival adaptation (McEwen, 1998).

Hypervigilance—a hallmark of anxiety—arises when the **amygdala**, the brain's fear center, becomes hypersensitive to threat cues. This heightened sensitivity contributes to:

- Startle responses to minor or neutral stimuli
- Difficulty relaxing or sleeping due to constant scanning
- Persistent over-analysis and anticipatory worry
- Inability to access cues of safety even in calm environments

In individuals with complex trauma, adverse childhood experiences, or chronic stress exposure, the **neuroception of safety** becomes impaired. Neuroception, as defined by Porges (2011), refers to the nervous system's subconscious detection of threat or safety. When this system is skewed, the brain remains locked in a hyper-alert state, even when no real danger is present.

Chronic overactivation of the HPA axis also contributes to:
- Impaired immune function
- Digestive dysfunction
- Mood instability
- Cognitive fog

- Hormonal disruption

From an NSI perspective, anxiety is not irrational—it is **misplaced activation** rooted in a body that has learned to expect threat. The goal of intervention is not to suppress or avoid anxiety, but to discharge the survival energy stuck in the system and restore capacity for a wider Window of Tolerance.

NSI emphasizes that healing begins with **respecting the body's logic**. Hypervigilance is not a flaw—it is an imprint. By approaching it with somatic compassion, we make room for presence, flexibility, and regulation.

Case Study 1: "Jamal" – Hypervigilance and Somatic Containment

Presenting Concern:
Jamal, a 32-year-old Black male, presented with chronic anxiety, sleep disturbance, and difficulty concentrating. He described himself as "always on edge" and reported frequent physical symptoms including jaw tension, elevated heart rate, and gastrointestinal discomfort. He had a history of growing up in a high-crime urban environment and was exposed to repeated community violence throughout adolescence.

Initial Assessment:
Jamal's baseline autonomic state indicated a chronic sympathetic activation pattern—marked by hypervigilance, shallow breathing, rapid speech, and frequent startle responses. He reported a constant internal narrative of scanning for danger, even in neutral or safe environments. Despite working in a secure office setting, he found himself unable to relax or feel safe.

NSI Intervention:
Interventions began with **visual orienting** and **extended exhale breathwork** to downregulate his system. A combination of **box breathing** and **environmental safety drills** (naming five safe

things in the room) were introduced as daily rituals. Over time, **interoceptive tracking** (particularly heartbeat and temperature mapping) increased Jamal's ability to identify his physiological signals of escalation.

He also engaged in **somatic boundary work**, exploring where "yes" and "no" lived in his body through weight-shifting and hand placement exercises. These embodied boundaries helped reduce his anticipatory activation in social settings.

Outcome:
After eight sessions, Jamal reported fewer panic symptoms, more restful sleep, and increased ability to remain present at work. He was able to identify early signs of sympathetic charge and use grounding tools before spiraling into full anxiety cycles. Most notably, he began initiating conversations with peers without excessive over-preparation or fear of judgment.

Clinician Note Summary:
Jamal's anxiety was not rooted in irrational thought—it was a nervous system loop conditioned by chronic exposure to threat. The NSI approach reframed his experience from "something wrong with me" to "my body is protecting me." By addressing the physiology first—through breath, safety mapping, and interoception—he built a new baseline of safety from the body up.

Interoceptive Awareness and Sensory Anchoring

Interoception is the internal perception of physiological signals—heartbeat, breath rhythm, hunger cues, muscle tension, body temperature, and more. It is the foundation of embodied self-awareness, helping us interpret what our bodies are experiencing in real time. In regulated states, interoception allows us to respond appropriately to our needs—resting when tired, eating when hungry, soothing when distressed.

However, under chronic anxiety, trauma, or persistent

hypervigilance, interoceptive awareness often becomes **disrupted or muted**. Many people report being "disconnected" from their bodies, unaware of hunger or exhaustion, or feeling emotionally overwhelmed without being able to identify where it's coming from. This disconnect is not a flaw—it is a **protective adaptation**. When the body has historically been a source of pain, shame, or danger, the nervous system may minimize awareness of internal cues as a survival strategy.

In culturally marginalized populations, particularly in BIPOC communities, this disconnection may be compounded by societal messages that devalue emotional expression and bodily intuition. For example, cultural norms that reward emotional stoicism or "pushing through pain" may inadvertently reinforce hypo-awareness of internal states. Interoception, then, becomes not only a clinical issue—but a **culturally-informed healing practice** that invites us back into sacred relationship with the body.

Neurosomatic Intelligence (NSI) offers tools to gently restore interoceptive awareness by re-training the nervous system to listen inward **without overwhelm**. The goal is not to forcefully feel, but to **build capacity** for internal sensing with safety and curiosity.

Key NSI-informed practices include:
- **Heartbeat Tracking**
  Quietly tune into the subtle pulse in your chest, wrist, or fingertips. This anchors attention to the present and improves vagal tone.

- **Breath Counting**
  Notice the natural rhythm of your breath without altering it. Count each inhale and exhale for several cycles, building awareness without control.

- **Temperature Mapping**

Scan the body for areas of warmth, coolness, or neutrality. This sensory precision teaches the brain to reorient toward here-and-now data instead of abstract threat.

- **Weight Distribution Awareness**
  Feel the contact of your feet on the floor, or your hips and spine against the chair. This reaffirms physical grounding and spatial orientation.

- **Muscle Tone Sensing**
  Gently notice areas of tightness or ease in your body. Are your shoulders lifted? Is your jaw clenched? Simply noticing begins the unwinding.

These anchoring techniques help **recalibrate the interoceptive system**, especially in those who are accustomed to being "stuck in their head" or dissociated from bodily cues. As the nervous system re-learns that the body is a safe place to inhabit, individuals often experience increased emotional clarity, improved regulation, and enhanced presence.

Importantly, these practices should be **titrated and consensual**. For those with complex trauma, rushing into deep interoception can trigger overwhelm. Slow pacing, permission to pause, and culturally responsive guidance are essential in creating environments where the body can be safely reclaimed.

Interoception is not just a neurological function—it is a **sacred portal to wholeness**. As we restore our capacity to feel from within, we restore trust in the body's wisdom, rebuild agency, and reconnect with the present moment. This inner anchoring becomes the groundwork upon which emotional resilience, somatic regulation, and deep self-compassion are built.

Case Study 2: "Maria" – Hypoarousal, Shutdown, and Rebuilding Presence

Presenting Concern:
Maria, a 47-year-old Latina woman, sought therapy for what she described as "emotional numbness and constant fatigue." She reported a long-standing inability to feel joy or connection, describing life as if she were "watching from a distance." Her trauma history included childhood emotional neglect and a recent divorce after 20 years of an emotionally unavailable marriage.

Initial Assessment:
Maria demonstrated signs of **dorsal vagal dominance**—slow speech, flat affect, low tone of voice, and difficulty accessing bodily sensation. She was often unsure how she felt in a given moment and struggled to make decisions. When asked where she felt her emotions, she responded, "I don't know—I don't feel much of anything."

NSI Intervention:
Sessions began with **relational orienting** and **gentle co-regulation** using voice tone, soft eye contact, and rhythmically paced language. **Micro-movements** (wiggling toes, shifting posture) were introduced to bring awareness to safe parts of the body. Over time, Maria was guided through **interoceptive practices** such as noticing breath depth, temperature differences across the skin, and subtle internal shifts.

As her somatic capacity grew, Maria began to describe her internal state with more clarity. She explored **weight-bearing exercises** and **movement-based tracking** to reinhabit her body. Introducing **vagal toning techniques** like humming and diaphragmatic breathing helped stimulate ventral engagement.

Outcome:
By session ten, Maria was initiating check-ins with herself multiple times a day, journaling sensations, and making conscious choices based on her embodied state. Her voice became more animated, her posture more upright, and she

reported moments of genuine presence during interactions with her children. Maria described it as "feeling like I came home to myself."

Clinician Note Summary:
Maria's dissociation and emotional flatness were protective adaptations from a lifetime of relational deprivation. Through titrated NSI techniques, she gradually rebuilt interoceptive awareness and ventral vagal tone. This case illustrates that regulation is not just about calming—it is about reconnection. NSI gave Maria a somatic language to return to herself, gently and safely.

Case Study 3: "Amina" – The Push-Pull of Panic and Collapse

Presenting Concern:
Amina, a 29-year-old African American woman, presented with panic attacks, chronic muscle tension, and episodes of emotional shutdown. She described an "internal tug-of-war" between overreacting and emotionally disappearing. She reported intense anxiety in intimate relationships, followed by numbness and guilt when she distanced herself. She described this as "getting too close too fast, then needing to run."

Her history included early relational trauma, emotional parentification, and inconsistent caregiving, with periods of neglect and enmeshment. Amina had previously been misdiagnosed with bipolar disorder, though her mood shifts were directly tied to relational stressors and nervous system dysregulation.

Initial Assessment:
Amina's somatic baseline alternated between **sympathetic hyperarousal** (racing heart, intrusive thoughts, compulsive planning) and **dorsal vagal collapse** (disassociation, binge watching shows for days, dissociative fog). Her body exhibited **mixed autonomic signals**—tight jaw and clenched fists, followed by slumped posture and difficulty initiating

movement.

She expressed frustration over her inconsistency: "Some days I'm in control, other days I just disappear." She also had a pattern of high emotional reactivity followed by shame and withdrawal.

NSI Intervention:
The first priority was **nervous system mapping**—helping Amina track her personal markers of escalation and collapse. Using visual tools and body-based journaling, she began identifying the "early whispers" of both states: shallow breath and muscle bracing before panic, and heavy limbs and zoning out before shutdown.

She was introduced to **titrated somatic sequences**, alternating between **activation practices** (like joint compression, vocal toning, and gentle shaking) and **downregulation tools** (extended exhale breathing, visual orienting, weighted blanket grounding). **Interoceptive pairing** helped her distinguish between emotions and sensations, reducing cognitive confusion during nervous system swings.

In relational processing, Amina practiced **fawn-pattern rewiring** through boundary-mapping and reclaiming her "no" in safe role-play scenarios. Using **relational orienting and micro-expressions**, she increased her tolerance for intimacy and reduced the cycle of emotional flooding and withdrawal.

Outcome:
By session 12, Amina could intervene early in her panic-collapse loop. She described feeling more "centered and informed" by her body, not just hijacked by it. She initiated vulnerable conversations with her partner without retreating afterward and created daily "check-in rituals" to track her nervous system.

Amina no longer feared her emotional waves. Instead, she said, "I've learned how to move through them."

Clinician Note Summary:
Amina's case exemplifies the complexity of mixed autonomic states—especially in clients with relational trauma. Her panic-avoidance cycle was not due to emotional instability, but to a nervous system stuck oscillating between unsafety in connection and collapse from overwhelm. NSI practices allowed her to build interoceptive capacity and restore choice within the push-pull of dysregulation. Over time, Amina developed a felt sense of stability, becoming the self-led witness of her own internal shifts.

Breath and Safety Drills

Breath is one of the most accessible and powerful tools for nervous system regulation. It forms a **bidirectional bridge** between the body and the brain, offering direct access to autonomic pathways that govern our stress and safety responses. In anxious or hyperaroused states, the breath often shifts unconsciously—becoming rapid, shallow, held, or even unnoticed. This type of breath reflects and reinforces sympathetic dominance (fight-or-flight), keeping the nervous system stuck in survival mode.

Neurosomatic Intelligence (NSI) teaches that we can **intentionally reshape our breath patterns** to send signals of safety to the brainstem and shift the body out of defense. Unlike thought-based coping mechanisms, breath modulation creates a **bottom-up shift** in physiology that paves the way for psychological clarity and emotional regulation.

Key Breathwork Practices for Somatic Resilience

Each breath technique below is strategically designed to **support different nervous system needs** and capacities:
- **Extended Exhale Breathing**
  Inhale for 4 counts, exhale for 8. This ratio activates the parasympathetic nervous system via the vagus nerve,

slows the heart rate, and signals to the body: "We are safe enough to soften." Useful during acute anxiety or bedtime routines.

- **Box Breathing (4-4-4-4)**
  Inhale, hold, exhale, hold—all for 4 counts. This rhythm enhances vagal tone, builds containment, and promotes emotional stability. Often used by military and high-performance professionals for calm under pressure, it's equally effective for nervous system training in trauma recovery.

- **Humming, Chanting, or Vibrational Exhale**
  Practices such as humming, mantra, or audible sighs stimulate the vocal cords, activating the ventral vagus nerve and promoting limbic system calming. These are especially potent for clients from spiritual or indigenous traditions, where voice and vibration are already part of cultural expression.

- **Nasal and Diaphragmatic Breathing**
  Encouraging slow, nose-only breathing and expansion through the belly rather than the chest helps anchor breath in the **lower lungs**, where vagal endings reside. This not only slows the respiratory rate but improves oxygen efficiency and interoceptive awareness.

These techniques are **not one-size-fits-all**. In NSI, breath practices are titrated to the client's capacity, cultural background, and present state. Someone in deep hypoarousal may need energizing breath, while another in hyperarousal may need grounding techniques with shorter durations to avoid overwhelm. Practitioners are trained to assess and adapt in real time.

Safety Drills: Training the Threat Detection System

When the nervous system is chronically dysregulated, it loses the ability to **accurately assess safety**. Even neutral or positive stimuli may be perceived as threat. NSI incorporates **safety drills** that teach the brain and body how to notice—rather than assume—the absence of danger.

These practices support what we call **neuroception re-patterning**—retraining the automatic, unconscious scanning process that determines whether we're safe or in danger.

- **Visual Orienting**
  Slowly and gently scanning the room with your eyes, allowing the head and neck to turn. This maps the spatial environment and **reverses tunnel vision**, a common trauma response. Let the eyes land on soothing, familiar, or beautiful elements—plants, art, color, or light.

- **Self-Touch Anchoring**
  Placing one or both hands on the chest, belly, cheek, or thighs while exhaling. Gentle, supportive touch recruits the ventral vagal system and communicates presence, belonging, and calm. It can also restore a sense of **bodily ownership**, especially after dissociation.

- **Environmental Mapping**
  Naming five things you can see, four you can hear, three you can touch, two you can smell, and one you can taste or imagine. This multisensory check-in returns awareness to the **here and now** and grounds the mind-body system in reality. This is especially helpful during anxiety spikes or flashbacks.

These drills serve as **neurological micro-rehearsals of safety**. They may seem simple, but their impact is profound. Over time, they teach the nervous system how to **downshift from chronic hyperarousal** and widen its Window of Tolerance.

The goal is not to eliminate all stress or intensity—but to equip the system with the **tools and trust** to move through them without collapse.

Breath Is the Rhythm of Safety

Breath and orientation are the **first languages of the nervous system**. Before we could speak, we breathed. Before we could analyze or make meaning, we scanned our environment for safety. These tools are ancient, intuitive, and biologically hardwired. They do not require perfection, only **presence and practice**.

In reclaiming the breath and retraining the threat response, we give ourselves a gift: the ability to feel safe enough to live, connect, and rest. This is the foundation of somatic resilience. And it begins with one inhale—and the choice to exhale it slowly.

The Invitation to Presence

Anxiety is often framed as a problem to fix, suppress, or avoid. But within the **Neurosomatic Intelligence (NSI)** model, anxiety is neither weakness nor pathology—it is a **biological alarm system** signaling that the nervous system does not feel safe. It is not the enemy—it is the messenger. And like all messengers, anxiety becomes less threatening when we learn to listen.

The invitation is not to silence anxiety, but to **enter into relationship** with it. To notice the patterns of breath, posture, muscle tone, and thought that arise in its presence. To ask the body, gently and without judgment: *What are you protecting me from? What haven't I yet made safe?*

This is the sacred shift from **panic to presence**. Instead of spiraling into cognitive overwhelm or reacting from fear, we learn to orient, ground, and regulate. In doing so, we **expand the nervous system's capacity** to hold the unknown—to stay present even when the outcome is uncertain.

Each time we meet anxiety with awareness instead of avoidance, we are **rewiring the nervous system** toward safety. Each regulated breath, each moment of embodied stillness, becomes a signal: *You are not in danger anymore. You can rest here. You are safe enough now to live, love, and feel.*

Over time, presence becomes our baseline—not because fear disappears, but because it no longer drives our behavior. Safety becomes not just a goal—but a **felt sense we return to with increasing ease**.

> Your body is not betraying you.
> It is broadcasting.
> It is asking you to slow down, to anchor, to listen.
> NSI teaches us how.

A Path Forward

As we close this chapter, remember: anxiety is not a flaw—it is **a form of brilliance** from a body that learned how to survive. But you were not meant to live in survival. You were meant to **thrive in connection, clarity, and choice**.

In the next chapter, we will explore another misunderstood set of responses—**anger, reactivity, and self-sabotage**—and how even these seemingly disruptive patterns are rooted in the wisdom of your nervous system.

The work ahead is not about becoming someone new. It is about **returning to who you were before the world taught you to be afraid of your own body**.

Let us walk this path—breath by breath, sensation by sensation—toward deeper presence, embodied leadership, and nervous system sovereignty.

References

The goal is not to eliminate all stress or intensity—but to equip the system with the **tools and trust** to move through them without collapse.

Breath Is the Rhythm of Safety

Breath and orientation are the **first languages of the nervous system**. Before we could speak, we breathed. Before we could analyze or make meaning, we scanned our environment for safety. These tools are ancient, intuitive, and biologically hardwired. They do not require perfection, only **presence and practice**.

In reclaiming the breath and retraining the threat response, we give ourselves a gift: the ability to feel safe enough to live, connect, and rest. This is the foundation of somatic resilience. And it begins with one inhale—and the choice to exhale it slowly.

The Invitation to Presence

Anxiety is often framed as a problem to fix, suppress, or avoid. But within the **Neurosomatic Intelligence (NSI)** model, anxiety is neither weakness nor pathology—it is a **biological alarm system** signaling that the nervous system does not feel safe. It is not the enemy—it is the messenger. And like all messengers, anxiety becomes less threatening when we learn to listen.

The invitation is not to silence anxiety, but to **enter into relationship** with it. To notice the patterns of breath, posture, muscle tone, and thought that arise in its presence. To ask the body, gently and without judgment: *What are you protecting me from? What haven't I yet made safe?*

This is the sacred shift from **panic to presence**. Instead of spiraling into cognitive overwhelm or reacting from fear, we learn to orient, ground, and regulate. In doing so, we **expand the nervous system's capacity** to hold the unknown—to stay present even when the outcome is uncertain.

Each time we meet anxiety with awareness instead of avoidance, we are **rewiring the nervous system** toward safety. Each regulated breath, each moment of embodied stillness, becomes a signal: *You are not in danger anymore. You can rest here. You are safe enough now to live, love, and feel.*

Over time, presence becomes our baseline—not because fear disappears, but because it no longer drives our behavior. Safety becomes not just a goal—but a **felt sense we return to with increasing ease**.

> Your body is not betraying you.
> It is broadcasting.
> It is asking you to slow down, to anchor, to listen.
> NSI teaches us how.

A Path Forward

As we close this chapter, remember: anxiety is not a flaw—it is **a form of brilliance** from a body that learned how to survive. But you were not meant to live in survival. You were meant to **thrive in connection, clarity, and choice**.

In the next chapter, we will explore another misunderstood set of responses—**anger, reactivity, and self-sabotage**—and how even these seemingly disruptive patterns are rooted in the wisdom of your nervous system.

The work ahead is not about becoming someone new. It is about **returning to who you were before the world taught you to be afraid of your own body**.

Let us walk this path—breath by breath, sensation by sensation—toward deeper presence, embodied leadership, and nervous system sovereignty.

References

- Craig, A. D. (2002). How do you feel? Interoception: the sense of the physiological condition of the body. *Nature Reviews Neuroscience, 3*(8), 655–666. https://doi.org/10.1038/nrn894

- Farb, N. A. S., Segal, Z. V., & Anderson, A. K. (2013). Attentional modulation of primary interoceptive and exteroceptive cortices. *Cerebral Cortex, 23*(1), 114–126. https://doi.org/10.1093/cercor/bhr385

- Khalsa, S. S., Adolphs, R., Cameron, O. G., Critchley, H. D., Davenport, P. W., Feinstein, J. S., ... & Paulus, M. P. (2018). Interoception and mental health: a roadmap. *Biological Psychiatry: Cognitive Neuroscience and Neuroimaging, 3*(6), 501–513. https://doi.org/10.1016/j.bpsc.2017.12.004

- McEwen, B. S. (1998). Stress, adaptation, and disease: Allostasis and allostatic load. *Annals of the New York Academy of Sciences, 840,* 33–44. https://doi.org/10.1111/j.1749-6632.1998.tb09546.x

- Porges, S. W. (2011). *The Polyvagal Theory: Neurophysiological foundations of emotions, attachment, communication, and self-regulation.* W. W. Norton & Company.

- Price, C. J., & Hooven, C. (2018). Interoceptive awareness skills for emotion regulation: Theory and approach of Mindful Awareness in Body-Oriented Therapy (MABT). *Frontiers in Psychology, 9,* 798. https://doi.org/10.3389/fpsyg.2018.00798

- Thayer, J. F., Åhs, F., Fredrikson, M., Sollers III, J. J., & Wager, T. D. (2012). A meta-analysis of heart rate variability and neuroimaging studies: Implications for heart rate variability as a marker of stress and health. *Neuroscience & Biobehavioral Reviews, 36*(2), 747–756. https://doi.org/10.1016/j.neubiorev.2011.11.009

CHAPTER 6

Anger, Reactivity, and Self-Sabotage

Rage as a Nervous System Protector

Anger is often misunderstood as a problem to manage, repress, or avoid. But from a Neurosomatic Intelligence (NSI) perspective, anger—especially rage—is not inherently destructive. It is protective. It emerges from the nervous system's impulse to defend, assert, and survive when boundaries have been violated or unmet needs have been chronically suppressed.

In Somatic Experiencing, Peter Levine (1997) identifies rage as a biological survival response. When a threat cannot be escaped, and the body's attempts to flee or fight are thwarted, that energy becomes frozen. Over time, that suppressed defensive activation can surface as chronic irritability, explosive outbursts, or internalized shame. Rage, then, is not dysfunction—it is **unmet action**. It is the body's cry for a boundary that was never allowed.

Bessel van der Kolk (2014) similarly describes how trauma disrupts the natural completion of the fight response, leaving the individual suspended in cycles of dysregulation. In these states, anger may be misdirected or suppressed altogether, turning inward as depression or self-sabotage. Robert Sapolsky's work on stress (2004) adds that prolonged activation of the stress response—especially when paired with helplessness—can further impair impulse regulation, heighten reactivity, and compromise executive function.

Viewed through this lens, rage is not a moral failure—it is a **neurobiological feedback signal**. It tells us: Something needs to be addressed. Something was not protected.

NSI Practices to Reclaim Healthy Aggression

In Neurosomatic Intelligence, **aggression is not equated with violence**—it is understood as life-force energy directed toward action, protection, and vitality. Healthy aggression allows us to advocate for ourselves, defend our boundaries, and move forward with purpose. Trauma, however, often distorts this relationship. It teaches the body that aggression is dangerous, shameful, or unsafe. As a result, individuals may suppress this energy, express it destructively, or lose contact with it altogether.

Reclaiming healthy aggression involves restoring the body's right to act. NSI draws from somatic modalities to safely access and discharge the incomplete fight responses stored in the nervous system. This work is not about reenacting conflict—it is about **reconnecting to power without collapse or explosion**.

Core NSI Practices Include:

1. Somatic Assertion Drills
Practicing safe, contained physical gestures—such as pushing against a wall, pressing hands together, or stomping—can activate the neuromuscular pathways associated with boundary-setting and defense. These movements help individuals feel what it's like to say "no" or "stop" with their full body engaged.

2. Boundary Mapping and Gesture
Exploring the physical expression of limits through movement (e.g., extending an arm out to indicate space, stepping backward to assert distance) helps rewire the body's instinctive capacity for self-protection. These gestures are often paired with verbal

boundary practice for integration.

3. Channeling Energy into Movement
Dynamic movement like hitting a cushion, primal shaking, expressive dance, or drumming provides safe outlets to move aggressive energy out of the body. The goal is to discharge activation without harming self or others, while retaining a sense of control and groundedness.

4. Vagal Tonification with Vocalization
Sound-based techniques—such as growling, humming, or forcefully exhaling while making noise—can tone the vagus nerve and provide a release for emotional tension. These methods help transition the body from sympathetic charge to ventral vagal restoration.

5. Repatterning Social Engagement
Since many individuals fear rejection or punishment for expressing anger, NSI encourages practice in relational safety. This can include role-play, co-regulation with a partner, or sharing frustration in a therapeutic setting while remaining attuned and connected.

A Note on Cultural and Gendered Layers

It is important to acknowledge that **anger has not been socially permitted equally**. In many communities, especially among Black, Indigenous, Latinx, and marginalized populations, expressions of anger are often met with disproportionate consequences. Similarly, gender norms have historically cast feminine anger as hysteria or immaturity, while celebrating masculine aggression as strength.

For these reasons, reclaiming anger is not just somatic work—it is cultural healing. It asks us to validate anger as a **human** experience, not a dangerous one, and to create environments where safe, embodied expression is honored, not policed.

Clinical Vignette: Reclaiming the Right to Say "No"

Client: *"Leila"*, 42-year-old Afro-Caribbean woman

Presenting Issue: Chronic people-pleasing, somatic shutdown in conflict, persistent fatigue, and resentment in personal relationships.

Background:
Leila came into NSI-informed therapy reporting overwhelming exhaustion, difficulty asserting herself, and a deep fear of disappointing others. Raised in a household where obedience was expected and dissent punished, she learned early that compliance was safer than confrontation. Over the years, this survival strategy hardened into a pattern of self-silencing, leading to chronic muscle tension, digestive issues, and emotional numbness. Every time she attempted to express a need or boundary, she felt a wave of shame, freeze, and a lump in her throat.

Therapeutic Process:
Our work began with nervous system mapping—tracking how her body responded to perceived conflict. Leila noticed a freeze response in her chest and shoulders anytime she imagined disappointing someone. She described this sensation as a "choking stillness."

Together, we introduced **assertion drills** using somatic resourcing. In one session, Leila practiced pushing against a yoga wall while vocalizing "No" in a steady, grounded tone. At first, she cried—grieving how long she had held this energy in. Over time, she began to report a growing sense of strength in her arms and warmth in her belly after each session.

We layered in **vagal toning techniques** using vocal exhale (such as humming and low growling) to discharge sympathetic charge. She paired this with breath regulation and **micro-boundary practices** in daily life: pausing before saying yes, naming one preference each day, and maintaining eye contact during low-stakes conversations.

Breakthrough Moment:
During a family gathering, Leila was asked to host an event with no notice. Instead of the automatic yes, she paused, placed a hand on her sternum, took a breath, and said, "I can't do that right now." Her voice was clear. Her body didn't collapse. For the first time, she felt safe in her "no."

Clinician Notes:
Leila's case exemplifies how somatic safety must precede behavioral change. Her chronic "fawning" wasn't a flaw—it was a dorsal vagal survival strategy. By restoring agency through body-based assertion, breathwork, and co-regulated practice, she reclaimed access to healthy aggression. Her boundary wasn't a rupture—it became a ritual of self-trust.

Preventing Emotional Hijacking

Emotional hijacking occurs when the nervous system becomes so dysregulated that executive function—particularly in the prefrontal cortex—goes offline. In this state, individuals may yell, shut down, overreact, or behave in ways that feel uncontrollable or misaligned with their values. These moments aren't character flaws—they are *neurobiological hijacks* driven by unresolved survival energy and a system overwhelmed beyond its Window of Tolerance.

The Neurobiology of a Hijack

When a perceived threat—emotional, relational, or environmental—is registered, the amygdala rapidly assesses for danger. If a threat is detected (even if it's emotional, like rejection), it signals the hypothalamus and brainstem to initiate a fight, flight, or freeze response. This floods the system with stress hormones like cortisol and adrenaline, bypassing the slower, more rational processing of the prefrontal cortex (Goleman, 1995; Sapolsky, 2004). The result? We say or do something in reactivity before we have the chance to choose a conscious response.

Common Signs Of Emotional Hijack:

- Sudden yelling, crying, or shutting down
- Feeling like you're "watching yourself from the outside"
- Inability to access language or rational thought mid-conflict
- Regret or shame immediately after reacting
- Emotional flashbacks or sense of "being 5 years old again"

NSI Practices to Prevent Hijacking:

Rather than aiming for perfection, NSI builds the *capacity* to recover faster and reduce the frequency of hijack episodes through the following methods:

1. Pre-Event Regulation
Before entering high-stakes situations (conversations, family events, deadlines), NSI encourages:

- Grounding drills (weighted blanket, feet on the floor)
- Box breathing (4x4x4x4)
- Micro-orienting (scanning the space for safe cues)
  This preemptively lowers arousal and expands the Window of Tolerance.

2. Titration and Pendulation
When intensity rises, the body must not be flooded. Titration means breaking big emotions into digestible doses. Pendulation

helps shift awareness between discomfort and safety:
"Can I feel this tension in my chest *and* notice the steadiness of the ground beneath me?"

3. Somatic Time-Outs
Stepping away is not avoidance—it is a strategy. Taking a moment to breathe, stretch, or regulate the body (even mid-conversation) allows the nervous system to recalibrate.

4. Repair Rituals
When hijacks happen (because they will), NSI emphasizes *somatic repair*:

- Name the state ("I noticed I was overwhelmed and went into shutdown.")

- Regulate together ("Can we take a breath together before we continue?")

- Offer safe touch or presence (if appropriate)
  This re-teaches the body that rupture is survivable—and that connection can be restored.

Integration with the Literature:

- **Peter Levine** emphasizes that incomplete survival responses (e.g., repressed fight or flight) increase the likelihood of hijacks. He recommends discharge through somatic movement and safe container-building (Levine, 1997).

- **Sapolsky** explains how chronic stress reduces hippocampal volume and impairs regulation of the HPA axis, leading to more frequent stress reactivity (Sapolsky, 2004).

- **Van der Kolk** discusses how trauma impairs time perception and emotion regulation, making hijacks feel like reliving the original wound (Van der Kolk, 2014).

From Hijack to Healing – Reclaiming Healthy Aggression

Anger is not the enemy. It is a signal. A compass. A call for boundaries, change, or protection. And when met with shame or suppression, it does not disappear—it mutates. It burrows into the body as inflammation, depression, reactivity, or chronic self-sabotage. But when honored through the lens of Neurosomatic Intelligence (NSI), anger becomes a powerful ally for transformation.

The goal is not to eliminate anger, but to *liberate it*—to reclaim its wisdom and direct its energy toward healing, advocacy, and alignment. Reactivity is what happens when our system is overwhelmed. Healthy aggression is what emerges when our system is supported.

As we've explored, emotional hijacking is not a personal failure—it is a physiological reality for systems under chronic threat. Through nervous system literacy, breath regulation, titration, co-regulation, and repair, we begin to unhook from reactive cycles and step into embodied choice.

You are not too much. You are not broken. You are carrying intelligent, unfinished biological stories that are longing to be completed. Every time you pause instead of explode, breathe instead of numb, repair instead of retreat—you are reshaping your nervous system and rewriting your legacy.

References
- **Levine, P. A. (1997).** *Waking the Tiger: Healing Trauma.* North Atlantic Books.

- **Levine, P. A. (2010).** *In an Unspoken Voice: How the Body Releases Trauma and Restores Goodness.* North Atlantic Books.

- **Porges, S. W. (2011).** *The Polyvagal Theory: Neurophysiological Foundations of Emotions, Attachment, Communication, and Self-Regulation.* W. W. Norton & Company.

- **Sapolsky, R. M. (2004).** *Why Zebras Don't Get Ulcers: The Acclaimed Guide to Stress, Stress-Related Diseases, and Coping.* Henry Holt and Company.

- **van der Kolk, B. A. (2014).** *The Body Keeps the Score: Brain, Mind, and Body in the Healing of Trauma.* Viking.

- **Ogden, P., Minton, K., & Pain, C. (2006).** *Trauma and the Body: A Sensorimotor Approach to Psychotherapy.* W. W. Norton & Company.

- **Siegel, D. J. (2012).** *The Developing Mind: How Relationships and the Brain Interact to Shape Who We Are.* Guilford Press.

- **Schore, A. N. (2003).** *Affect Regulation and the Repair of the Self.* W. W. Norton & Company.

CHAPTER 7

Fawn Response, Attachment, and Boundaries

The Nervous System Behind People-Pleasing

In trauma-informed spaces, the "fawn response" is gaining recognition as the lesser-discussed but equally protective sibling to fight, flight, and freeze. Often labeled as "people-pleasing" or "codependency," the fawn response is not a flaw in personality—it is a *neurobiological adaptation to relational threat*.

When a child grows up in an environment where emotional needs are met inconsistently—or where love is conditional, unstable, or abusive—their nervous system learns that safety is not found in autonomy, but in *appeasement*. The instinct to resist or withdraw might be too dangerous. Instead, the body encodes a survival strategy centered on compliance, emotional caretaking, and hyper-attunement to others' moods.

Fawning behaviors can include:

- Anticipating and managing the emotions of others at your own expense

- Chronic self-abandonment or disconnection from preferences, needs, and desires

- Over-apologizing or taking responsibility for others' feelings

- Feeling guilt or fear when setting boundaries

- Adapting identity to fit the perceived expectations of others

Neurosomatically, the fawn response is governed by a blend of **sympathetic arousal** (hypervigilance and tracking threat) and **dorsal vagal shutdown** (muting one's own needs and impulses). This creates a patterned nervous system state where appeasement becomes the perceived path to connection, belonging, and survival.

Over time, this embodied strategy creates a dissonance between internal truth and external behavior. The body may comply, but the soul begins to ache. Exhaustion, resentment, and anxiety often emerge—not because of weakness—but because the system is *over-functioning in service of safety*.

Importantly, the fawn response is not limited to early trauma. It can be reactivated in adulthood during emotionally unsafe relationships, high-stakes work environments, or systems of oppression that demand conformity to survive. This is especially true in marginalized communities, where cultural survival often requires the suppression of voice, anger, and personal boundaries.

From an NSI perspective, the goal is not to shame the fawning response—but to honor its origin and *retrain the system to trust in authentic, reciprocal connection*. Through somatic repatterning, individuals can learn to:

- Recognize when their system is defaulting to appeasement

- Reconnect with internal signals of preference, discomfort, and "no"

- Anchor into self-worth and safety without requiring external validation

- Build the capacity to tolerate boundary-setting, even when it feels unsafe

Reclaiming one's voice and needs is not selfish—it is *a nervous system reclamation of sovereignty*. And it begins by understanding that people-pleasing is not a personality trait. It is a body's way of staying alive.

Codependency as a Nervous System Survival State

Codependency is often pathologized as a relational dysfunction rooted in low self-esteem, enmeshment, or lack of boundaries. But beneath these surface behaviors lies a deeper truth: **codependency is a nervous system adaptation to early and chronic relational insecurity**.

In Neurosomatic Intelligence (NSI), we view codependency not as a character flaw, but as a *learned survival pattern* —an embodied response to environments where love, safety, or acceptance were conditional on caretaking, compliance, or invisibility.

Many individuals who develop codependent tendencies come from homes where:

- Emotional expression was punished, invalidated, or ignored

- Boundaries were routinely violated or never modeled

- Caregiving roles were reversed, with children parenting themselves

- Connection was tethered to performance, perfectionism, or peacekeeping

In these contexts, the nervous system learns: *"My worth is based on how well I manage others."* This creates an internalized belief that love must be earned through self-sacrifice, emotional labor, or abandonment of authentic needs.

Neurobiologically, codependency reflects **chronic sympathetic arousal** coupled with **low interoceptive awareness**. The body becomes hyper-focused on monitoring others for threat, mood changes, or rejection cues, while simultaneously suppressing its own internal signals of exhaustion, resentment, or "no." Over time, this leads to:

- Difficulty identifying personal needs and preferences

- Guilt when receiving or resting

- Compulsion to fix, rescue, or manage others' emotions

- Anxiety or fear of abandonment when asserting boundaries

- Self-worth dependent on being needed

From a regulatory standpoint, the codependent pattern is *high-effort survival*. It costs the nervous system significant energy to maintain connection through control, appeasement, or over-functioning. And yet, it feels safer than the perceived danger of being alone, rejected, or forgotten.

NSI addresses codependency by retraining the nervous system to *decentralize others and re-center self*. This includes:

- **Interoceptive Reconnection**: Helping clients identify and honor their internal cues of discomfort, desire, or depletion

- **Boundary Mapping**: Teaching the body to feel the

difference between "mine" and "not mine" somatically

- **Attachment Repair**: Exploring safe, reciprocal relationships that do not require self-abandonment to maintain connection

- **Regulation Without Rescue**: Building tolerance for others' distress without enmeshing or overextending

As clients begin to reclaim self-reference and regulate their own nervous system, a profound shift occurs. Care no longer requires control. Love no longer requires loss of self.

Codependency, when understood through the lens of survival, invites compassion—not condemnation. The nervous system was doing its job: *protecting you through connection*. Now, with support and somatic tools, you can learn that safety does not have to cost your sovereignty.

Somatic Boundary Practices: Reclaiming the Felt Sense of Self

Boundaries are not just verbal declarations—they are embodied experiences. Before we can say "no" with our voice, we must *feel* our "no" in the body. In the Neurosomatic Intelligence (NSI) model, boundaries are understood as somatic signals of selfhood: the capacity to sense where you end and others begin.

For individuals with fawn adaptations or codependent tendencies, boundaries often feel dangerous or inaccessible. This is not due to weakness or passivity, but to **nervous system imprinting**. If earlier experiences taught the body that setting limits leads to rejection, punishment, or abandonment, the nervous system will default to compliance as a safety strategy.

To shift this pattern, NSI focuses not on behavioral scripts alone, but on **repatterning the body's physiological relationship with boundaries**. This means building a felt sense of safety in saying "no," receiving "no," and discerning where one's energy, responsibility, and emotional labor begin and end.

Core Somatic Boundary Practices In Nsi

1. **The "Yes" and "No" Body Scan**
   Clients are guided to recall a time when their body felt an authentic "yes" and a true "no." They then scan for the physical sensations associated with each—tightening, opening, contraction, warmth, withdrawal. This builds interoceptive fluency for boundary discernment.

2. **Containment Visualization**
   Using imagination and felt sense, clients envision a protective boundary (e.g., a bubble, light, fabric, wall) surrounding their body. This visualization, repeated with breath and grounding, strengthens the somatosensory perception of personal space.

3. **Arm Extensions and Push-Away Movements**
   Physically practicing the gesture of pushing something away (with breath and intention) engages musculature and proprioception to reinforce the boundary reflex. This can be profoundly empowering for individuals who tend to collapse or freeze in boundary violations.

4. **Boundary Titration in Relationships**
   Clients begin to experiment with low-stakes "no's" or unmet needs in real time while tracking nervous system responses. They might say, "I need a moment before I respond," or "I'm noticing I'm getting tired, can we pause?" The goal is not perfection—it's capacity-building through incremental challenge.

5. **Grounding and Completion After Boundary Setting**
   Post-boundary repair is crucial. Clients learn to downshift after setting a limit through grounding, orienting, shaking, or breathwork. This teaches the body that conflict does not equal danger—and that it is safe to remain in the body even when rupture occurs.

Why Somatic Boundary Work Matters

From a neurobiological perspective, boundary setting requires access to the **ventral vagal system** (social engagement and connection), paired with **sympathetic mobilization** (assertiveness). Many trauma survivors are either too dorsal (collapse, freeze, appease) or hyper-sympathetic (rage, shutdown after conflict) to access this integrated state. Somatic practices create the internal scaffolding to access a *regulated assertiveness*—where saying "no" is not a rupture, but a return to self.

Boundary work is not just about relationships—it is about identity. The more we feel our own edges, the more we can show up in our truth without apology or collapse. Over time, these embodied practices build the foundation for healthier attachment, empowered communication, and reciprocal connection.

Attachment Wounds and Reparenting Pathways

Our earliest relationships lay the blueprint for how we relate to ourselves and others. These formative dynamics shape not only our psychological framework but also our **nervous system wiring**—what feels safe, what feels threatening, and what we must do to be accepted, loved, or merely tolerated.

When caregivers are inconsistent, unavailable, intrusive, or unsafe, the nervous system adapts. It may learn to overfunction (anxious attachment), emotionally detach (avoidant attachment), or collapse into disorganized patterns of craving and fearing connection at once. These attachment wounds are not cognitive flaws—they are *neurobiological survival strategies*, developed before we had language or choice.

In the **Neurosomatic Intelligence (NSI)** model, attachment wounds are seen as disruptions in **co-regulation and self-attunement**. Rather than pathologize these adaptations, NSI invites a process of **compassionate reparenting**—not through abstract affirmations, but through *embodied safety and consistent neural rewiring*.

Understanding the Embodied Imprint of Attachment

Attachment trauma is stored in the body. It shows up in:
- **Startle or shutdown during emotional intimacy**
- **Clinging to connection, even when harmful**
- **Over-identifying with caregiving roles while neglecting self**
- **Shame spirals after setting boundaries**
- **Inability to trust calm or safety—it feels unfamiliar**

These are not signs of failure. They are echoes of earlier strategies that once protected you. But they are not required anymore.

Reparenting Through the Body: NSI Pathways

Reparenting is not about replacing our parents. It is about **offering the safety, validation, and consistency that our younger self never received—through present-day nervous system practices.**

Here are core NSI tools used to rewire attachment patterns:

1. Titrated Self-Attunement
Start small. Clients practice noticing internal cues (e.g., "I feel tired," "I'm hungry," "I need quiet") and responding to them with validation and care—mirroring what an attuned caregiver would offer. This builds **interoceptive trust**.

2. Inner Child Resourcing
Clients visualize or dialogue with their younger self during moments of dysregulation. Somatic anchors such as touch (hand over heart), gentle rocking, or wrapped containment help restore a **felt sense of safety** in the present.

3. Co-Regulation Repatterning
Rather than avoiding or clinging to connection, clients learn to **co-regulate** with safe others through eye contact, vocal tone, breath matching, or presence. This builds trust in relational repair and nervous system flexibility.

4. Repairing After Relational Rupture
Clients are guided to notice what happens *after* conflict or boundary setting. Do they spiral into shame? Collapse into silence? NSI helps clients **track and interrupt the internalized punishment loop** by offering regulating practices post-rupture—like orienting, breathwork, and affirming self-touch.

5. Somatic Reparenting Rituals
Clients develop daily rituals that provide safety, consistency, and nurturing. These can include self-holding practices, affirmations while grounding, warm baths, walks in nature, or creating sacred space for reflection. Over time, these rituals send the message: *You are safe, worthy, and allowed to exist exactly as you are.*

From Survival Bonds to Secure Attachment

When attachment wounds are left unexamined, they become **survival bonds**—we stay connected out of fear, obligation, or trauma reenactment rather than mutual respect or joy. Through NSI and reparenting, we shift the nervous system's expectation of relationship from *threat* to *sanctuary*.

This isn't about perfect healing—it's about progressive capacity. The more often we show up for ourselves with compassion, clarity, and care, the more our body learns that it is safe to attach, express, and receive.

We do not heal attachment wounds in theory—we heal them in the **living tissue** of embodied practice.

From Appeasement to Authenticity

The fawn response is not a flaw—it is a form of brilliance born from necessity. When fight or flight were not options, your nervous system chose the only path that preserved attachment and reduced harm: appeasement. What once kept you safe may now keep you small, silenced, or stuck in codependent loops that erode your authenticity.

But survival patterns are not life sentences. Through Neurosomatic Intelligence, we learn to rewire the story in the body—not by shaming old responses, but by **honoring the intelligence that created them** and gently building new ones.

As you reclaim your boundaries, your voice, and your nervous system sovereignty, you step out of roles you were never meant to play—caretaker, peacekeeper, emotional sponge—and into who you truly are: *connected, embodied, whole.*

You are not here to constantly manage others' comfort.

You are here to belong to yourself.

The NSI path reminds us that healing is not about becoming less sensitive—it is about becoming **more attuned**, more anchored, more able to stand in your truth without fear of rupture. With each breath, each boundary, and each act of reparenting, you are teaching your body: *I am safe now. I do not* *have to disappear to be loved.*

This is not a return to who you were before trauma. It is the arrival of who you were always meant to be.

References

- **Bowlby, J. (1988).** *A secure base: Parent-child attachment and healthy human development.* Basic Books.

- **Fisher, J. (2017).** *Healing the fragmented selves of trauma survivors: Overcoming internal self-alienation.* Routledge.

- **Levine, P. A. (2010).** *In an unspoken voice: How the body releases trauma and restores goodness.* North Atlantic Books.

- **Maté, G. (2003).** *When the body says no: Exploring the stress-disease connection.* Wiley.

- **Ogden, P., Minton, K., & Pain, C. (2006).** *Trauma and the body: A sensorimotor approach to psychotherapy.* W. W. Norton & Company.

- **Porges, S. W. (2011).** *The polyvagal theory: Neurophysiological foundations of emotions, attachment, communication, and self-regulation.* W. W. Norton & Company.

- **Rothschild, B. (2000).** *The body remembers: The psychophysiology of trauma and trauma treatment.* W. W. Norton & Company.

- **Schore, A. N. (2012).** *The science of the art of psychotherapy.* W. W. Norton & Company.

- **Van der Kolk, B. A. (2014).** *The body keeps the score: Brain,* *mind, and body in the healing of trauma.* Viking.

SECTION III: RECONNECTION AND REPATTERNING

CHAPTER 8

Co-Regulation and Relational Healing

The Human Nervous System Is Wired for Connection

From the moment we are born, our nervous system is shaped by the presence—or absence—of attuned connection. Long before we understand language, we understand tone. Before we grasp logic, we feel presence. Connection is not a luxury—it is a biological imperative. It is the first language we speak, and the foundation upon which our sense of safety and self is built.

Neurosomatic Intelligence (NSI) recognizes co-regulation as a foundational principle of healing. While self-regulation is vital, the ability to regulate *with* another is the original blueprint of emotional safety. Babies cannot self-soothe; they co-regulate through eye contact, heartbeat rhythm, skin-to-skin touch, and vocal tone. These interactions are not merely nurturing—they are neurological training grounds. They shape how the developing brain wires itself for attachment, stress response, and emotional expression.

This early relational wiring is referred to as **social synaptogenesis**—the process through which neural pathways are formed based on social interaction. Studies in infant neuroscience demonstrate that mutual gaze, vocal attunement, and physical proximity activate the ventral vagal system, promoting physiological regulation and emotional bonding (Schore, 2001; Porges, 2011).

When co-regulation is consistent and safe, the nervous system develops flexibility, resilience, and trust. The child learns that stress can be soothed, needs can be met, and relationships can be a source of safety. This lays the groundwork for healthy attachment, impulse control, and self-worth.

But when co-regulation is absent, inconsistent, or frightening, the system adapts for survival. These adaptations may include hypervigilance, avoidance, dissociation, or compulsive self-reliance. While protective in the short term, these patterns often come at the cost of intimacy, vulnerability, and authentic connection. In adulthood, they may manifest as difficulties in trusting others, struggles with emotional intimacy, or an overdependence on control.

NSI teaches that these are not personality flaws or signs of emotional weakness—they are brilliant survival strategies written into the nervous system. And with enough safety, presence, and practice, these patterns can be rewritten. The nervous system is not static—it is plastic. Which means healing, connection, and re-patterning are always possible.

The Science of Co-Regulation: Polyvagal Foundations

According to Dr. Stephen Porges' Polyvagal Theory (2011), the autonomic nervous system is composed of three hierarchical circuits, each associated with a different survival strategy:

- **Ventral Vagal Pathway (Social Engagement):** This is the newest and most evolved branch of the vagus nerve, responsible for connection, calm, play, and relational safety. It supports our ability to attune, empathize, and regulate with others.

- **Sympathetic Nervous System (Mobilization):** This branch activates the fight-or-flight response when a threat is detected. It mobilizes energy to escape danger but inhibits connection and higher-order reasoning.

- **Dorsal Vagal Pathway (Immobilization):** The oldest branch, it triggers freeze or shutdown when escape is impossible. It conserves energy but leads to dissociation, numbness, and isolation.

Polyvagal Theory emphasizes that these pathways are not just reactive—they are relational. Co-regulation specifically activates the **ventral vagal system**, the biological platform of trust, attunement, and presence. When another person offers steady eye contact, a warm voice, or calm body language, it sends cues of safety to our brainstem —*before* we ever consciously interpret the situation.

This is called **neuroception**—the nervous system's subconscious evaluation of safety and threat.

This is why healing in isolation can be so difficult. Our physiology responds not only to thoughts or insight, but to *relational cues*. Without consistent signals of safety from others, the nervous system remains locked in protection mode—even if we cognitively want to heal.

In Neurosomatic Intelligence, co-regulation is not viewed as dependency—it is seen as **the biological norm**. It is how we are wired to regulate, repair, and thrive. By understanding these pathways, practitioners can intentionally create relational environments that restore ventral vagal tone and teach the body that connection can be safe again.

This foundation sets the stage for deeper work with attachment, trust, boundaries, and emotional intimacy— each of which will be explored in the following sections.

Attachment Through a Neurosomatic Lens

Attachment theory has long described patterns of connection formed in early caregiving relationships: secure, anxious, avoidant, and disorganized. Neurosomatic Intelligence builds on this by asking a critical question:

What nervous system adaptations

created this attachment style?

- **Secure attachment** reflects a regulated nervous system that experienced consistent, attuned co-regulation. Safety was modeled, mirrored, and internalized.

- **Anxious attachment** often develops when connection was inconsistent or unpredictable—activating a state of hypervigilance and emotional amplification to maintain proximity and gain approval.

- **Avoidant attachment** may emerge when emotional expression was met with rejection, dismissal, or overwhelm—leading the nervous system to downregulate connection in favor of autonomy and emotional suppression.

- **Disorganized attachment** arises in environments where caregivers were both a source of comfort and fear—fragmenting the nervous system's ability to organize around a coherent strategy for connection and safety.

These attachment patterns are not moral failures—they are somatic blueprints. They reflect the body's brilliant attempts to survive in environments where safety was not consistently available. NSI affirms that these patterns, while once protective, can now be lovingly rewired.

This requires more than intellectual insight. It requires *experiential re-patterning* at the level of the nervous system. Through practices that provide steady cues of relational safety—such as co-regulated breath, attuned presence, and polyvagal-informed communication—new neural associations are formed.

It's not enough to cognitively understand that we have an insecure attachment style. The nervous system must be given **new experiences** of safety, responsiveness, and trust.

In NSI, we do not shame the protector strategies—we

thank them. And then we show the body, over and over again, that it is safe to soften, connect, and be seen.

Rupture, Repair, And The Path To Trust

All relationships experience rupture. What matters most is not perfection, but the capacity for repair. From a nervous system perspective, repair is how we rebuild safety after a break in connection.

When rupture is ignored, minimized, or punished, the nervous system encodes the relationship as unsafe. The memory of disconnection becomes a threat imprint, reinforcing hypervigilance, withdrawal, or emotional shutdown in future interactions. But when repair includes vulnerability, accountability, and regulation, it creates a corrective experience. It strengthens connection, restores relational trust, and widens the Window of Tolerance.

"Rupture is inevitable. Repair is relational mastery."

Practicing relational repair involves:

- **Regulating yourself before responding**: Soothing your own system so you can show up with presence, not reactivity.

- **Naming the impact without blame**: Focusing on how you felt, rather than attacking the other person.

- **Listening with curiosity rather than defense**: Staying open to understanding the other's perspective, even when it's uncomfortable.

- **Offering or receiving acknowledgment**: Naming harm or misunderstanding, and allowing space for empathy.

- **Reconnecting through co-regulation**: Using tone, breath, eye contact, or appropriate touch to re-establish a sense of shared safety.

This cycle teaches the nervous system that relationships can be safe even after conflict. That safety is not the absence of rupture—it is the presence of return. In fact, frequent and successful repairs are one of the strongest predictors of resilient relationships.

In NSI-informed practice, repair becomes a daily ritual—a commitment to relational hygiene. It's not about never messing up. It's about creating enough safety, regulation, and emotional fluency to return after the rupture and grow stronger because of it.

Trauma's Impact on Connection

For those with complex trauma, co-regulation can feel foreign—or even threatening. If early experiences taught the body that connection leads to pain, abandonment, or control, the nervous system may equate closeness with danger. In such cases, even the desire for intimacy may be met with unconscious resistance.

This shows up as:

- Flinching from touch or closeness
- Shutting down during emotional conversations
- Difficulty trusting even supportive people
- Choosing isolation over vulnerability
- Feeling overwhelmed by empathy or compassion

From an NSI standpoint, these are not flaws in character. They are nervous system strategies for survival. They are protective adaptations shaped by lived experience, biology, and memory encoded through the body—not willful resistance.

Healing in this context must be slow, relational, and deeply respectful of the body's timing. NSI does not push connection—it builds **capacity** for it through incremental, titrated doses of safe relational exposure. This may begin with co-regulating with a practitioner, pet, or even nature. It may look like practicing eye contact for a few seconds, allowing a supportive touch, or simply noticing another person's calm breath without shutting down.

Over time, these micro-experiences of safety accumulate. They form new neural pathways and interrupt the old equation that says, "Closeness = danger." Instead, the body begins to learn: "Closeness can feel safe. I can stay. I can soften."

Through this gentle, body-led approach, NSI helps individuals rewrite the relational blueprint—moving from self-protection to mutual connection. And in that process, they begin to reclaim the birthright of attuned, nourishing, and sustainable relationship.

Polyvagal Communication: Speaking the Language of Safety

The nervous system reads how we say things before it processes what we say. This is why **tone of voice, facial expression, body posture, and eye contact** are central to relational safety.

In Neurosomatic Intelligence, we teach a practice called **Polyvagal Communication**—a method of using body-based signals to foster connection, trust, and regulation in interpersonal interactions. It is especially powerful in roles such as caregiving, leadership, therapy, education, and parenting.

Key principles include:

- **Softening the face and jaw**: A tense or rigid face signals stress or aggression. A relaxed expression communicates calm and openness.
- **Speaking from a grounded breath**: When we breathe low and slow, our voice carries tones of safety. Shallow or constricted breath often results in tight, high-pitched vocal tones that can signal anxiety or threat.

- **Using open gestures**: Avoid crossed arms or closed body language. Hands visible, palms open, and body slightly turned toward the other communicates receptivity.
- **Slowing down the rhythm and cadence**: Rapid speech can activate the sympathetic nervous system. Slowing down helps signal calm and gives the listener space to process.

These subtle shifts cue the other person's **ventral vagal system**, inviting them into a co-regulated state. They tell the body: *You're safe. You're seen. You're not alone.*

Practicing Polyvagal Communication is not about performance—it's about presence. It trains us to embody the very safety we wish to create for others. In doing so, we become relational anchors—not by what we say, but by how we say it.

This form of nervous system-informed communication transforms not only personal relationships but professional environments. It invites us to lead, love, and listen in ways that speak directly to the body's deepest longing: **to feel safe in connection.**

Somatic Tools for Relational Healing

To build co-regulation capacity, NSI practitioners use a range of somatic tools that engage the body's social engagement system and promote trust, safety, and presence in relational dynamics:

- **Mirroring**: Subtly reflecting another's posture, breath rate, or facial expression to build unconscious rapport. This technique activates the mirror neuron system and promotes a felt sense of being understood. Over time, this fosters attunement and signals that "we are in sync," reducing feelings of loneliness or alienation.
- **Synchronized breathing**: Co-breathing with

another person in a slow, regulated rhythm helps entrain both systems to a state of calm. Whether through silent breathing or guided breathwork, this practice supports heart rate variability and invites parasympathetic restoration.

- **Relational orienting**: Gently noticing and appreciating safe features of the other (such as their eyes, tone, or presence) to orient the nervous system toward connection instead of threat. This can include pausing to name what feels warm, grounding, or inviting about the other person. When practiced mindfully, it anchors the brainstem in the present moment and reduces reactive loops.

- **Touch calibration**: Exploring safe, consensual forms of touch—such as hand squeezes, warm hugs, or a hand on the back—while tracking the nervous system's response. Practitioners help individuals discern when touch feels comforting versus overstimulating. This not only builds tolerance for closeness, but re-educates the nervous system that touch can be safe, soothing, and mutual.

These practices help both individuals shift from **guardedness to groundedness**. They cultivate the neurobiological conditions necessary for vulnerability, empathy, and repair.

Importantly, these tools must always be guided by **consent, titration, and mutual regulation**. The goal is not to bypass discomfort but to expand tolerance for connection, one embodied moment at a time.

When practiced regularly, these somatic tools don't just change behavior—they change the *nervous system's default settings.* Over time, they rewire us for deeper intimacy, clearer boundaries, and relational resilience that is rooted in the body, not just the mind.

Healing Happens In Connection

Healing is not a solo pursuit. It is deeply relational. While self-regulation is essential, it is only one side of the healing equation. The other is co-regulation—the ability to be seen, supported, and soothed by others.

Our culture often glorifies hyper-independence and emotional stoicism. Yet neuroscience tells a different story: *resilience is relational.* The human nervous system evolved in community, wired to survive through connection, not isolation. Our biology depends on safe bonds, attuned presence, and reciprocal care.

In the NSI model, healing is not about becoming self-sufficient to the point of exclusion—it is about cultivating the capacity to receive. To let love in. To allow another nervous system to meet ours in moments of fear, grief, joy, or pain.

Every time we are met with attunement in a moment of dysregulation, our nervous system learns: *I can bring my whole self here. I will not be punished for feeling. I am safe to belong.*

This is why relational healing is so powerful. It doesn't just change our thoughts—it rewires our biology. It restores our trust. It teaches us that we are not too much, not too broken, and never alone.

NSI offers a framework to practice this daily: through nervous system hygiene, polyvagal communication, relational rituals, and co-regulatory care. These are not luxuries—they are lifelines. Through them, we build relational resilience that endures.

Because in the end, healing becomes not only sustainable—but shared.

References
- **Cacioppo, J. T., & Patrick, W. (2008).** *Loneliness: Human*

Nature and the Need for Social Connection. W. W. Norton & Company.

- **Cozolino, L. (2014).** *The Neuroscience of Human Relationships: Attachment and the Developing Social Brain* (2nd ed.). W. W. Norton & Company.

- **Levine, P. A. (2010).** *In an Unspoken Voice: How the Body Releases Trauma and Restores Goodness.* North Atlantic Books.

- **Ogden, P., Minton, K., & Pain, C. (2006).** *Trauma and the Body: A Sensorimotor Approach to Psychotherapy.* W. W. Norton & Company.

- **Porges, S. W. (2011).** *The Polyvagal Theory: Neurophysiological Foundations of Emotions, Attachment, Communication, and Self-Regulation.* W. W. Norton & Company.

- **Schore, A. N. (2001).** The effects of early relational trauma on right brain development, affect regulation, and infant mental health. *Infant Mental Health Journal,* 22(1-2), 201–269.

- **Siegel, D. J. (2012).** *The Developing Mind: How Relationships and the Brain Interact to Shape Who We Are* (2nd ed.). The Guilford Press.

- **Siegel, D. J. (2020).** *The Power of Showing Up: How Parental Presence Shapes Who Our Kids Become and How Their Brains Get Wired.* Ballantine Books.

- **van der Kolk, B. A. (2014).** *The Body Keeps the Score: Brain, Mind, and Body in the Healing of Trauma.* Viking.

- **Wallin, D. J. (2007).** *Attachment in Psychotherapy.* The Guilford Press.

CHAPTER 9

Building Somatic Resilience and Emotional Agility

From Regulation to Resilience

Healing the nervous system does not end at regulation—it evolves into resilience. While regulation helps us shift from dysregulation into balance, **resilience is the capacity to stay grounded in the face of disruption** and return to center more quickly and fluidly. It is the difference between surviving stress and *growing* through it.

Regulation is the foundation. It offers moment-to-moment strategies to restore safety in the body, such as breathwork, vagal stimulation, or grounding exercises. But **resilience is the architecture** built on that foundation—a dynamic capacity for *nervous system agility* that enables us to stay connected to our values, intuition, and relational clarity even when life is hard.

In this context, **emotional agility** refers to our ability to move *through* emotions, rather than bypass or suppress them. It is not about being unaffected by grief, anger, or fear—it is about embodying these emotions with presence and allowing them to complete their biological cycle. When we are emotionally agile, we can:

- Experience grief without being consumed by it
- Express anger without harming ourselves or others
- Navigate uncertainty without collapsing into panic
- Stay open to joy and connection, even after betrayal or

loss

Neurosomatic Intelligence (NSI) is not just a method of trauma resolution. It is a **neurobiological framework for personal evolution**. It teaches us that resilience is not about toughness—it is about *flexibility*. A resilient nervous system can mobilize when needed, rest when safe, and stay relational under pressure. It is not bound by rigid defenses or frozen in old patterns.

NSI helps cultivate what neuroscience calls **neuroplasticity**—the brain and nervous system's ability to form new connections and adapt. This adaptability becomes embodied through daily regulation rituals, sensory integration, interoceptive awareness, and relational safety. In short, it is how we become *more of ourselves*—not despite our past, but because we have learned to move through it, reclaim our story, and root into the present.

In the pages ahead, we will explore:
- The biological mechanics of stress and resilience

- Why recovery—not perfection—is the heart of nervous system health

- How to create rituals that fortify your baseline state

- Somatic practices that train your system to become more fluid, less reactive, and more empowered

Because resilience is not something you chase—it is something you *become*. Through presence. Through practice. Through the radical remembrance that your body is not a problem to solve—it is the source of your strength.

What Is Somatic Resilience?

Somatic resilience is the body's ability to remain

regulated, responsive, and coherent under stress. It is rooted in nervous system capacity—not personality, willpower, or mindset alone. A resilient system can experience activation (sympathetic arousal) without losing access to connection and grounding (ventral vagal tone).

Resilience is not about avoiding stress or pain—it's about expanding your ability to hold intensity without fragmenting. It is the capacity to engage with life's challenges while staying anchored in safety, agency, and embodied presence.

The Three Pillars of Somatic Resilience

In the NSI model, resilience is built in layers that correspond to biological and experiential development:

1. **Physiological Regulation** – These are the foundational rhythms of your body. Practices like intentional breathwork, nervous system nourishment (hydration, whole foods), restorative sleep, movement, and sunlight all support baseline nervous system tone. Without physiological balance, higher-level emotional regulation is compromised.

2. **Emotional Literacy** – This is the ability to *feel and name* what is happening inside without collapsing into it or pushing it away. Emotional literacy includes skills like emotional tracking, using descriptive rather than judgmental language, and normalizing emotional variability. The more familiar you are with your emotional range, the less threatening intensity becomes.

3. **Somatic Capacity** – This refers to the nervous system's ability to tolerate increasing levels of sensation, relational closeness, or emotional charge without reverting to shutdown, overdrive, or dissociation. It includes working with boundaries, discomfort, and embodied self-trust. Building somatic capacity

involves titration—slowly increasing exposure to internal states that were previously overwhelming.

Each of these layers is *trainable*. And when cultivated intentionally, they work synergistically to create a deeply resilient, embodied foundation for navigating life's stressors.

The Science of Stress Adaptation

Stress itself is not inherently negative. In fact, **eustress**—a term for positive stress—is essential for learning, growth, and motivation. It helps us rise to challenges, sharpen focus, and build confidence. However, when stress becomes **chronic, unrelenting, or overwhelming**, it can dysregulate the nervous system and deplete our adaptive capacity over time.

At the center of the stress response is the **HPA axis** (hypothalamic-pituitary-adrenal), a hormonal feedback loop that governs how the body mobilizes in response to threat. When a challenge is perceived, the HPA axis triggers the release of cortisol and other stress hormones to prepare the body for action. In a healthy system, once the threat passes, this response deactivates and returns to baseline.

But in a dysregulated system—especially one shaped by trauma, systemic stress, or prolonged adversity—this return to baseline is disrupted. The result is **allostatic load**: a cumulative burden of stress that leads to elevated cortisol levels, disrupted sleep cycles, weakened immunity, inflammation, and emotional instability (McEwen, 1998).

This is why **recovery** is more important than avoidance. A resilient nervous system isn't one that never gets triggered—it's one that knows how to **come back to regulation**. That's where NSI comes in.

The NSI Pathway: Top-Down Meets Bottom-Up

Neurosomatic Intelligence supports stress adaptation by targeting both **top-down** and **bottom-up** mechanisms:

- **Top-Down Pathways**: These include cognitive approaches like mindfulness, reappraisal, and attention training. They help increase meta-awareness and redirect attention from threat-based loops.

- **Bottom-Up Pathways**: These involve body-based practices such as breath regulation, vagal nerve toning, somatic tracking, and sensory grounding. These tools work directly with the limbic system and autonomic pathways to reduce physiological reactivity.

By integrating both approaches, NSI enhances **neuroplasticity**—the nervous system's ability to adapt and learn. It also strengthens **interoceptive awareness**, which is key to detecting early signals of stress and responding before overwhelm occurs.

Ultimately, NSI builds a resilient feedback loop: *stimulus → awareness → regulation → recalibration*. And the more this loop is practiced, the stronger and more flexible the nervous system becomes.

Daily Rituals for Nervous System Resilience

Resilience is not a trait—it is a daily *practice*. Just like physical strength is built through repetition, **nervous system resilience is developed through consistency**. In the NSI model, we teach nervous system hygiene routines that progressively build capacity, flexibility, and quicker recovery over time.

These rituals are not about adding more to your to-do list. They are intentional nervous system deposits that build inner reserves of calm, clarity, and strength. When practiced regularly, they rewire your baseline state, shifting your system toward greater balance and responsiveness.

Examples of NSI-Informed Daily Rituals

1. **Morning Orienting Rituals**
   - Start your day by signaling safety to the nervous system.
   - Practices include visual tracking (following a moving object with your eyes), body scanning (gently noticing and naming sensations from head to toe), and grounding exercises like placing both feet on the floor with intention.
   - These techniques help establish a ventral vagal tone from the beginning of the day, preparing your body for presence and flow.

2. **Midday Regulation Breaks**
   - Take 3–10 minute breaks to reset your nervous system.
   - Tools include box breathing, gentle spinal movement, vagal toning techniques (like humming or gargling), or simply stepping outside and engaging with nature.
   - These breaks discharge accumulated sympathetic charge and support cognitive clarity for the rest of the day.

3. **Evening Downshift Protocols**
   - Train your system to transition from activation to restoration.
   - Include practices like candle-gazing, journaling three things you're grateful for, progressive muscle relaxation, or rocking motions that cue safety.
   - These rituals enhance sleep quality by signaling the body that it is safe to rest.

4. **Boundary Mapping Exercises**

- Develop embodied awareness of your limits by practicing somatic "yes" and "no" responses.
- Use imagery, posture shifts, or voice to explore what agreement and discomfort feel like in your body.
- This builds confidence in interpersonal boundaries and reduces nervous system overwhelm in social interactions.

These rituals don't just regulate—they **build capacity**. Over time, they reshape how your nervous system meets challenge, responds to change, and moves through adversity. They create the inner architecture for becoming someone who doesn't just *cope* with stress, but transforms it into growth.

Emotional Agility: Navigating the Inner Landscape

Emotional agility is the nervous system's ability to move fluidly between emotional states without getting stuck, hijacked, or overwhelmed. It is not about avoiding hard emotions—it is about *metabolizing* them in a way that promotes growth, clarity, and coherence.

Rather than being driven by reactivity, emotional agility is built on self-awareness, body-based presence, and the ability to tolerate emotional intensity. This allows us to stay grounded in our values and relationships—even when we feel disrupted.

Key Skills of Emotional Agility

- **Tracking Internal Shifts with Curiosity**: Paying attention to bodily sensations, thought patterns, and breath rhythm as clues to our emotional landscape.
- **Titrating Emotional Intensity**: Meeting big emotions in small doses so they do not overwhelm the system. This includes pausing, regulating, and allowing space before full expression.
- **Practicing Somatic Expression**: Using movement, voice,

posture, and breath to move emotional energy through the body. This supports emotional completion rather than suppression.

- **Anchoring into Regulation**: Returning to breath, grounding tools, or co-regulation to remain present with the emotion rather than being hijacked by it.

In NSI, emotional agility is not a performance—it's a *felt skill*. It means being able to stay in relationship with yourself even when emotions are intense. To honor the message behind the emotion while staying rooted in your body.

Over time, this practice builds:
- **Inner Trust**: You learn that emotions are not dangerous, but data.
- **Psychological Flexibility**: You become more adaptive and less reactive.
- **Somatic Integration**: You embody a wider range of emotional experience without losing access to self-regulation.

Emotional agility turns emotional waves into vehicles of transformation. It is how we reclaim our humanity—not by perfecting our emotional responses, but by relating to them with compassion, movement, and presence.

Your Resilient Self Is Not Ahead—It Is Within

Resilience is not a destination. It is not found in some future version of yourself where pain no longer touches you. Rather, **resilience is the presence you bring to your pain**—the breath you take in the middle of chaos, the softening of your shoulders when tension rises, the return to yourself after being pulled away by stress, fear, or shame.

In Western culture, resilience is often misunderstood as toughness, stoicism, or grit. But from a **neurosomatic perspective**, resilience is tenderness. It is responsiveness. It is the capacity to feel deeply without drowning, to face difficulty without losing coherence, and to rise again—not because you bypassed your pain, but because you met it with presence.

NSI teaches that the body is not a barrier to healing—it is the **portal**. Our nervous system is the map and the medicine. When we regulate first, we can repattern beliefs. When we build capacity, we expand possibility. And when we come home to the body, we remember that **who we are is enough—not someday, but now.**

The Resilient Self Is:

- **Rooted in the body**, not abstract ideals

- **Shaped by regulation**, not performance

- **Grown through practice**, not perfection

- **Expressed through embodiment**, not just mindset

Through daily nervous system hygiene, emotional tracking, and relational repair, we don't become someone new—we become *more of who we already are*. Resilience is not about escape from suffering. It is about **meeting life fully, and knowing that you are equipped to face it**.

Each time you orient to safety, each time you pause before reacting, each time you allow an emotion to move through without judgment—you are laying the neural groundwork for sovereignty.

You are not fragile.
You are not broken.
You are building a nervous system that can hold joy, grief, rage, desire, and still remain whole.

This is the essence of somatic resilience. Not a fixed state, but a living relationship with your body, your breath, and your truth.

So let go of chasing the "healed" version of yourself.
Return instead to the self who is here—breathing, becoming, enough.
Because your resilient self is not ahead. **It is already within.**

References

Cozolino, L. (2016). *The neuroscience of psychotherapy: Healing the social brain* (3rd ed.). W. W. Norton & Company.

David, S. (2016). *Emotional agility: Get unstuck, embrace change, and thrive in work and life.* Avery.

Levine, P. A. (2010). *In an unspoken voice: How the body releases trauma and restores goodness.* North Atlantic Books.

McEwen, B. S. (1998). Protective and damaging effects of stress mediators. *New England Journal of Medicine, 338*(3), 171–179. https://doi.org/10.1056/NEJM199801153380307

Porges, S. W. (2011). *The polyvagal theory: Neurophysiological foundations of emotions, attachment, communication, and self-regulation.* W. W. Norton & Company.

Siegel, D. J. (2010). *The mindful therapist: A clinician's guide to mindsight and neural integration.* W. W. Norton & Company.

Van der Kolk, B. A. (2014). *The body keeps the score: Brain, mind, and body in the healing of trauma.* Viking.

CHAPTER 10

Body Relationship, Eating, and Gut Health

The Body Was Never the Enemy: Reclaiming a Trust-Based Relationship with Self

In a culture that profits from disconnection, especially disconnection from the body, many of us learn to mistrust our hunger, resent our curves, and silence our instincts. But beneath body image struggles, disordered eating, and compulsive movement patterns lies a deeper wound—a nervous system shaped by shame, survival, and sensory confusion.

Body dysmorphia, binge eating, and restriction are not simply habits or willpower issues. They are somatic survival strategies. For many, the body became a battleground long before food ever entered the picture. These patterns often originate in early experiences of trauma, neglect, control, or attachment rupture, where the body was either hyper-scrutinized or entirely ignored.

When the nervous system is in a prolonged state of dysregulation, **food, body image, and movement become tools to soothe, control, or express unmet needs.** The brain tries to regulate chaos through control or excess. The gut-brain connection—via the vagus nerve—further complicates this, as our enteric nervous system plays a central role in both emotional and physical digestion.

In this chapter, we explore how Neurosomatic Intelligence (NSI) reframes body-based behaviors through the lens of neurobiology and compassion. We unpack:

- The roots of dysmorphia, binge-restrict cycles, and compulsive exercise

- The science of the gut-brain axis and its role in interoceptive clarity

- Somatic practices to restore food safety, body trust, and digestive resilience

The body is not a problem to fix—it is a partner to honor. And when we begin to **listen to the body as an ally**, not an adversary, we create space for healing that goes far beyond nutrition or aesthetics. We begin the sacred work of reinhabiting ourselves.

Body Dysmorphia, Binge Patterns, and Restriction as Survival Strategies

Body image struggles are often pathologized as vanity, discipline issues, or psychological disorders. But when we view these behaviors through a Neurosomatic Intelligence (NSI) lens, we uncover a more compassionate truth: **these patterns are the nervous system's attempts to create control, safety, or agency in a world that once felt unpredictable or dangerous.**

Body Dysmorphia: Perception Distorted by Protection

Body dysmorphia isn't just a distorted view in the mirror—it's a neurobiological defense. When the nervous system has been shaped by trauma, especially trauma that involved **violation, neglect, criticism, or objectification**, the brain may begin to dissociate from the body or develop obsessive focus on perceived flaws as a way to "fix" or control what feels uncontainable.

In many clients, this shows up as:
- A hyper-focus on weight, size, or specific body parts

- Inability to register physical changes even after weight loss or muscle gain

- Chronic self-comparison and negative self-talk

- Oscillation between perfectionism and disgust

From a somatic perspective, **this is not narcissism—it's fragmentation.** When your body becomes the scapegoat for unprocessed emotional pain, it's easier to fixate on your thighs than to face what those thighs once carried. NSI helps guide clients back to the present body—not through forced affirmations, but through gentle interoceptive reconnection and trauma-informed embodiment.

Binge Patterns: Seeking Soothing, Not Shame

Binge eating is often misunderstood as a lack of willpower or indulgence. In reality, it is often the body's attempt to **soothe a dysregulated nervous system** that has been living in depletion, stress, or emotional starvation.

Biologically, binge patterns often follow periods of restriction or high stress. Elevated cortisol increases cravings for high-fat, high-sugar foods. The parasympathetic system may try to self-soothe through dopamine-seeking behaviors like eating, especially after extended sympathetic overdrive.

Psychologically and somatically, bingeing can serve as:
- A grounding mechanism after dissociation

- A way to *feel full* after chronic emotional emptiness

- A form of rebellion against chronic control or perfectionism

- A signal flare from the body saying, "I need comfort, not punishment"

NSI reframes bingeing as a **communication**, not a character flaw. By building daily somatic safety and supporting the body's regulation rhythms, clients often find that their urges soften—not through restriction, but through resourcing.

Restriction: Control in the Face of Chaos

Food restriction can create a temporary sense of power and certainty—especially for individuals who grew up in environments where their bodies, needs, or autonomy were not respected. Calorie counting, food rules, excessive fasting, or compulsive exercise may become coping strategies to establish a sense of control in the body when the world feels overwhelming.

This pattern is often praised in Western culture as "discipline" or "fitness," making it especially insidious and difficult to dismantle. But the nervous system's signature is clear:

- Hyperarousal or freeze before meals

- Anxiety around hunger cues

- Avoidance of pleasure, softness, or rest

- Overreliance on structure to feel emotionally regulated

Restriction is often the **flip side of hypervigilance**—it's not about health; it's about safety. NSI practices bring curiosity to the parts of us that cling to food control, offering new pathways to regulate without rigidity.

Cultural and Systemic Considerations

For marginalized populations—especially BIPOC

individuals, queer folks, and people socialized as women—body-based survival strategies are often reinforced by systemic oppression, cultural body norms, and intergenerational trauma.

- **Eurocentric beauty standards** disproportionately harm people of color by pathologizing natural body types.

- **Historical trauma** (e.g., slavery, colonization, forced sterilization) has disconnected many communities from food sovereignty and body autonomy.

- **Religious purity cultures** often link eating, pleasure, and body exposure with shame.

Understanding the **cultural somatics** behind these patterns is essential. Healing is not just individual—it's communal, ancestral, and political. NSI honors that **body reclamation is body liberation.**

Gut-Brain Axis and Interoceptive Recovery

The phrase "trust your gut" is more than a metaphor—it is a neurological reality. The gut and brain are in constant communication via the **vagus nerve**, forming a bidirectional feedback system known as the **gut-brain axis**. In Neurosomatic Intelligence (NSI), understanding this axis is foundational to healing trauma, restoring regulation, and rebuilding body trust.

The Science Behind the Gut-Brain Connection

The gut is home to over **100 million neurons**, often referred to as the "second brain" (Gershon, 1998). It produces over **90% of the body's serotonin** and plays a key role in regulating mood, immune function, digestion, and emotional resilience.

When the nervous system is dysregulated, the gut often suffers. This can show up as:

- Irritable Bowel Syndrome (IBS)
- Chronic bloating or indigestion
- Loss of appetite or emotional eating
- Gut pain without clear medical cause
- Nutrient absorption issues and food intolerances

Research shows that **early life stress** and unresolved trauma increase the likelihood of gut inflammation, altered microbiota, and visceral hypersensitivity (Mayer et al., 2015). Simply put: if you've had trauma, your gut has, too.

Trauma's Disruption of Interoception

Interoception is the nervous system's ability to perceive and interpret internal signals—like hunger, fullness, gut discomfort, or emotional tension in the belly. Trauma often **numbs** this awareness, leaving individuals disconnected from the body's cues. This can lead to:

- Ignoring hunger or satiety until extremes are reached
- Confusing emotional discomfort with physical need
- Eating without presence or sensation
- Fear or distrust of internal cues

From the NSI perspective, **rebuilding interoceptive awareness is core to gut healing.** Without this reconnection, even the best nutritional or probiotic protocols will feel disconnected or dysregulated.

Somatic Practices for Gut-Brain Healing

NSI includes a range of bottom-up tools to support vagal

tone, restore gut function, and reawaken interoceptive trust:
- **Vagal Toning Techniques**: Humming, gargling, chanting, and slow singing stimulate the vagus nerve and increase parasympathetic activity.

- **Belly-Based Breathwork**: Gentle diaphragmatic breathing restores gut motility and creates a sense of spaciousness in the torso.

- **Abdominal Mapping**: Mindful palpation and gentle massage of the stomach area improve proprioception and release muscular tension.

- **Mindful Eating Rituals**: Slowing down meals, chewing thoroughly, and checking in with the body before and after eating restore safety and presence in the digestive process.

- **Gut-Aware Journaling**: Tracking emotional states alongside digestive patterns helps identify nervous system triggers and relational correlations to gut flares.

These somatic tools do more than soothe symptoms—they retrain the nervous system to perceive the gut not as a source of threat, but as a reliable partner in regulation.

The Emotional Landscape of the Gut

In many cultures, the gut is considered the seat of intuition and emotional wisdom. We "stomach" bad news, feel "sick to our stomach," or "trust our gut." This language reflects the **deep entwinement of emotion and digestion.**

Unprocessed emotions—especially grief, fear, shame, and anger—often settle in the gut. In NSI practice, we support clients in exploring these sensations **not as dysfunction, but as data.** For example:

- A tight, clenched belly may signal held fear or bracing for impact.

- Chronic nausea may reflect unresolved disgust or boundary violations.

- Bloating may stem from a nervous system that is too constricted to digest effectively.

By bringing **gentle curiosity** to these sensations, we allow the gut to release not just food—but emotional residue, relational pain, and trauma memory.

The Gut as a Portal for Recovery

Restoring gut-brain coherence is about more than probiotics and digestive enzymes. It is about **rewriting the relationship** between your body, your emotions, your past, and your food. In NSI, gut healing is approached through:

- **Biological support** (nourishment, hydration, movement)

- **Somatic awareness** (sensation tracking, breathwork, tone)

- **Emotional attunement** (feeling what the gut has held)

- **Narrative repair** (releasing shame around eating, body, and digestion)

The gut doesn't just digest food—it digests life. Healing this center allows us to process more than meals. It helps us metabolize old stories, reclaim body trust, and feel safe in our own internal world.

Rewriting Movement and Food Safety

In trauma recovery, the way we move and the way we nourish ourselves are often imprinted by our survival patterns.

For many, movement and food are not neutral experiences—they are charged with control, punishment, shame, or fear. In Neurosomatic Intelligence (NSI), we aim to rewrite these associations by reconnecting the body to safety, choice, and joy.

Movement as a Narrative of Control or Liberation
Many trauma survivors associate movement with:
- **Punishment** (e.g., forced physical activity as discipline)

- **Obligation** (e.g., exercise only for weight loss or "earning" food)

- **Dissociation** (e.g., pushing through pain or ignoring body signals)

This creates a cycle where the body is either ignored, overexerted, or micromanaged—none of which promote nervous system regulation.

In NSI, we shift movement from a transactional act to a **relational ritual**. We ask not, *"What do I need to burn?"* but *"What does my body need to feel safe today?"*

Restorative movement practices include:
- **Gentle swaying or rocking** to soothe the vestibular system

- **Walking meditations** with somatic cue tracking

- **Stretching with interoceptive focus**, noticing sensations rather than form

- **Spontaneous or intuitive dance**, reclaiming joyful, expressive embodiment

This reorientation allows the nervous system to experience

movement as safety—not survival.

Over time, clients begin to choose movement not to fix the body, but to **befriend it**.

Food Safety Beyond Nutrition

Just as movement becomes distorted by trauma, so too does eating. For many, food has become:

- A **source of control** or rebellion

- A **comfort mechanism** during overwhelm

- A **trigger** for shame, guilt, or collapse

- A **battleground** for perfectionism, fear, or identity

Even "healthy eating" can become disordered when driven by anxiety, rigidity, or body hatred. In NSI, food is not moralized. It is treated as part of the relational ecosystem of the nervous system—a **source of information**, comfort, and repair.

Somatic Tools for Rebuilding Food Safety

To heal one's relationship with food, we begin not with calorie charts or macros—but with the **body's internal language**. NSI practices include:

- **Pre-Eating Check-ins**: Tuning into physical and emotional states before meals—Am I hungry, lonely, anxious, tired?

- **Slow Eating Rituals**: Using all five senses to ground in the eating experience; chewing fully and savoring textures, tastes, and sensations

- **Body-Led Portions**: Letting the body—not external rules—determine when to start, pause, or stop

- **Curiosity Over Control**: Replacing rigid thinking ("I

shouldn't eat that") with curiosity ("How does this make my body feel?")

- **Repairing Internal Dialogue**: Challenging internalized shame by practicing affirming thoughts like, "My body deserves nourishment," or "Eating is a form of care."

These practices rewire eating as a **co-regulatory experience**—one that increases presence, reduces guilt, and fosters trust in the body's cues.

Cultural and Ancestral Integration

Food and movement are deeply **cultural experiences**. For BIPOC communities, diet culture often promotes disconnection from ancestral foods and movement traditions. Healing must include **reclaiming and honoring cultural rituals**, such as:

- Traditional meals prepared with intention
- Dance, drumming, or martial arts as embodied practices
- Communal eating as connection and belonging

NSI practitioners are trained to incorporate **culturally responsive approaches** that validate these traditions instead of replacing them with Westernized wellness ideals. Reclaiming ancestral movement and nourishment is a form of **somatic decolonization**—a powerful act of healing and resistance.

A Return to Relational Nourishment

When we rewrite our relationship to food and movement, we are not just changing behaviors—we are **rebuilding intimacy with the body**. We shift from domination to dialogue, from punishment to partnership. The body becomes a source of truth, not a project to be managed.

In NSI, this return to relational nourishment is central. It asks:

- Can I trust my hunger?

- Can I move because it feels good, not because I must?

- Can I hear what my body needs without overriding it with shame or fear?

The answer is yes—and it begins with one breath, one bite, one step at a time.

Clinical Vignette: Reclaiming Nourishment After Trauma

Client Profile:
Name: Shanelle (pseudonym)
Age: 33

Presenting Concerns: Disordered eating patterns, chronic body shame, exercise compulsion, gastrointestinal distress

Background: Shanelle is a biracial woman with a history of childhood emotional neglect and sexual trauma during adolescence. She reports long-standing body dysmorphia and cycles of bingeing, restriction, and compulsive exercise. Recently, she began experiencing gut issues including bloating, cramping, and loss of appetite, which were exacerbated by stress.

NSI Process and Somatic Interventions:
Initial sessions focused on interoceptive awareness and building safety in stillness. Shanelle identified a fear of "stillness" as equivalent to "losing control"—a somatic imprint from childhood environments where chaos was constant and her body felt unsafe.

Using NSI techniques, Shanelle learned:
- **Breath-led body scans** to differentiate emotional from physical hunger

- **Sensory grounding during meals**, using smell and temperature awareness

- **Movement shifts**, replacing forced cardio with intuitive stretching, walking in nature, and short dance sessions

The somatic cue that marked her shift was subtle—one day, she paused mid-bite and noticed her stomach soften. She looked up and said, "This is the first time I've eaten without guilt in years."

Cultural Context:
With guidance, Shanelle also explored her maternal Caribbean roots and began incorporating ancestral foods that had previously been labeled "unhealthy" by Western diet culture. She described the experience of preparing a traditional meal with her grandmother as "healing in my bones."

Clinician Note:
Shanelle's recovery illustrates how trauma often hijacks our relationship to food and body movement. By restoring a sense of internal safety and incorporating culturally affirming practices, she was able to reframe nourishment as connection—not control. NSI helped her transition from body punishment to body partnership, highlighting the importance of ritual, relational safety, and gentle embodiment in the recovery process.

From Control to Connection

Our relationship with food, movement, and the body is often the most intimate—and the most wounded—terrain we navigate. For many, nourishment and embodiment have been shaped by trauma, shame, and systems of disconnection that taught us our bodies were not safe, not beautiful, or not worthy.

But the body is not the enemy. It is the archive of our survival. Every binge, every restriction, every compulsion to run, hide, or shrink is not a failure of willpower—it is a brilliant adaptation from a time when control was the only access to safety we had.

Neurosomatic Intelligence invites us to rewrite that story. By restoring interoceptive awareness, re-patterning how we move, and healing the gut-brain connection, we begin to reclaim relationship with the body—not as an object to discipline, but as an ally to listen to. This work is not about perfection. It is about presence.

To eat with reverence.
To move with joy.
To rest without guilt.
To inhabit your body like a home instead of a battlefield.
This is the healing.

Your body is sacred. And your healing is possible.

References

- **American Psychiatric Association. (2013).** *Diagnostic and statistical manual of mental disorders* (5th ed.). American Psychiatric Publishing.

- **Craig, A. D. (2002).** How do you feel? Interoception: the sense of the physiological condition of the body. *Nature Reviews Neuroscience, 3*(8), 655–666. https://doi.org/10.1038/nrn894

- **Kaye, W. H., Fudge, J. L., & Paulus, M. (2009).** New insights into symptoms and neurocircuit function of anorexia nervosa. *Nature Reviews Neuroscience, 10*(8), 573–584. https://doi.org/10.1038/nrn2682

- **Levine, P. A. (1997).** *Waking the tiger: Healing trauma.* North Atlantic Books.

- **Mayer, E. A. (2016).** *The mind-gut connection: How the hidden conversation within our bodies impacts our mood, our choices, and our overall health.* Harper Wave.

- **Porges, S. W. (2011).** *The polyvagal theory: Neurophysiological foundations of emotions, attachment, communication, and self-regulation.* W. W. Norton & Company.

- **Schore, A. N. (2003).** *Affect dysregulation and disorders of the self.* W. W. Norton & Company.

- **Siegel, D. J. (2010).** *The mindful therapist: A clinician's guide to mindsight and neural integration.* W. W. Norton & Company.

- **Turnbaugh, P. J., Ley, R. E., Mahowald, M. A., Magrini, V., Mardis, E. R., & Gordon, J. I. (2006).** An obesity-associated gut microbiome with increased capacity for energy harvest. *Nature, 444*(7122), 1027–1031. https://doi.org/10.1038/nature05414

- **Van der Kolk, B. A. (2014).** *The body keeps the score: Brain, mind, and body in the healing of trauma.* Viking.

CHAPTER 11
Peace, Rest, and Sleep Recovery

When Stillness Feels Unsafe: Understanding Sleep Resistance

For individuals with a history of trauma, hypervigilance, or chronic nervous system dysregulation, rest can paradoxically feel like a threat. While rest and sleep are biologically essential for healing and homeostasis, the experience of **stillness**—a slowed heartbeat, quiet environment, or disengagement from external stimuli—can signal danger to a dysregulated nervous system.

This is not a failure of willpower or self-discipline; it is a **neurobiological imprint** of survival. The **dorsal vagal shutdown** state (Porges, 2011) may have once been a protective response during overwhelming events, while hyperarousal states conditioned the body to stay on guard to avoid further harm. In such systems, silence is not soothing—it is associated with **isolation, abandonment, or threat**.

From the lens of Neurosomatic Intelligence (NSI), we understand that sleep resistance often arises from the **inability to downshift** into parasympathetic dominance. When the nervous system has learned that safety is conditional or inconsistent, it does not automatically allow deep rest. Instead, it remains in a loop of **subconscious scanning**, attempting to ensure survival by remaining alert, even during rest periods.

Common expressions of this include:
- Racing thoughts or catastrophic thinking at night

- A sense of dread or unease as bedtime approaches

- Sudden spikes in heart rate or muscle tension while lying down

- Avoidance of stillness through overstimulation (e.g., phone scrolling, late-night eating, or compulsive cleaning)

- A feeling of collapsing into sleep rather than gently drifting

These patterns are not irrational—they are the body's attempt to protect against perceived threats. Sleep, which requires surrender, can feel like exposure to danger when the **neuroception** of safety (Porges, 2011) has been compromised.

In NSI, we don't force rest. We **prepare the body for it** through titrated safety-building practices that gradually increase the system's tolerance for stillness. This includes:

- **Co-regulatory cues** that precede sleep (e.g., touch, rhythmic movement, soothing voice tones)

- **Ritualized downshifting** through patterned evening routines

- **Somatic anchors** that create continuity between waking regulation and rest (e.g., breath pacing, weight-based grounding)

- **Environmental adjustments** that reduce neuroceptive threat (soft lighting, warmth, scent, or familiar sound)

The path to rest begins with **nervous system permission**. When safety is embodied—not just conceptually understood—

stillness transforms from a threat into a sanctuary.

This reframing is essential for trauma survivors, neurodivergent individuals, and anyone navigating chronic stress. By meeting the body where it is—alert, on guard, and protective—we create the compassionate conditions for it to finally exhale.

Tools to Reclaim Parasympathetic Dominance

Parasympathetic dominance—the state in which the body rests, digests, heals, and regenerates—is the foundation of deep recovery and resilience. But for individuals with trauma, chronic stress, or hyperaroused systems, this state is often difficult to access, let alone sustain. The body may be stuck in **sympathetic overdrive** (fight/flight) or **dorsal vagal shutdown** (freeze/collapse), making it challenging to feel safe enough to truly rest.

In the **Neurosomatic Intelligence (NSI)** framework, reclaiming parasympathetic dominance is not about forcing relaxation. It's about creating the physiological and environmental conditions that invite the body to downshift gradually, safely, and consistently. This requires working with both **bottom-up (body-based)** and **top-down (cognitive)** pathways to reestablish a felt sense of safety.

Here are key NSI-aligned tools that support this transition:

1. Vagal Toning Practices
The vagus nerve—often referred to as the "rest and digest" superhighway—plays a central role in parasympathetic regulation. Stimulating the vagus nerve enhances vagal tone, promoting relaxation, emotional regulation, and resilience.

- **Humming or Chanting:** The vibration from vocal resonance stimulates the vagus nerve through the throat and chest cavity.

- **Gargling or Splashing Cold Water on the Face:** Stimulates cranial nerves connected to vagal pathways, activating calming responses.

- **Singing or Slow Melodic Breathing:** Uses vocal cords and controlled breath to soothe the nervous system.

2. Breath-Based Interventions

Breath is one of the most direct ways to shift autonomic state. In NSI, breathwork is approached not as performance, but as a *dialogue with the nervous system.*

- **Extended Exhale Breathing:** Inhale for 4 counts, exhale for 6–8. The long exhale increases parasympathetic activation and signals safety.

- **Diaphragmatic (Belly) Breathing:** Anchors the breath deep in the body, reducing shallow chest breathing associated with anxiety and threat.

- **Box Breathing (4-4-4-4):** Builds containment, presence, and capacity by balancing the nervous system.

3. Grounding Through Proprioception

Proprioceptive input helps the brain map the body in space, which promotes a sense of containment and physical safety.

- **Weighted blankets or body wraps** before sleep

- **Pressing feet firmly into the floor** or squeezing hands together rhythmically

- **Rocking or slow swaying** to soothe the vestibular system

- **Self-hugging or wrapping the arms across the chest**

4. Somatic Sleep Cues

When used consistently, these cues condition the nervous system to recognize bedtime as a signal of safety—not threat.

- **Consistent nighttime rituals** (e.g., tea, dim lights, specific music)

- **Scent-based anchors** like lavender, sandalwood, or chamomile

- **Guided body scans or NSI-based sleep scripts**

- **"Safe Touch" cues**, such as placing a hand on the heart or abdomen, paired with breath

5. Safety Through Environment

The external environment must match the internal cues of safety for downshifting to occur. NSI teaches practitioners and clients to co-create sleep environments that reduce stimulation and threat cues:

- **Sound:** Low-frequency, repetitive sounds (white noise, ocean waves, binaural beats)

- **Light:** Warm, dim lighting or red-spectrum light before sleep

- **Temperature:** Cool, consistent room temperature with warm tactile textures

- **Clutter reduction:** A tidy, predictable space supports a sense of internal order

Reclaiming parasympathetic dominance is not a one-time fix—it's a **daily devotion** to working with, not against, the body's rhythm. Each moment of safety reinforces a new pattern, replacing old survival strategies with embodied calm. Over time, the body learns: *Stillness is not dangerous. Rest is not collapse. Sleep* *is a return, not an escape.*

Nervous System Bedtime Rituals: Training the Body to Trust Sleep

Restful sleep is not simply a cognitive decision—it is a physiological surrender. For trauma survivors or individuals with chronic dysregulation, this surrender can feel deeply unsafe. Nervous system bedtime rituals are daily practices designed to cue the body toward **trust, containment, and downregulation.**

In the **Neurosomatic Intelligence (NSI)** framework, these rituals serve as anchors—repeating sensory, somatic, and relational signals that gently train the brain to recognize nighttime as safe.

These are not just habits—they are **neurobiological training grounds** for parasympathetic dominance.

1. The Power of Predictable Sequence

The nervous system thrives on predictability. A consistent, structured wind-down routine creates neurological safety by reducing surprise and increasing coherence.

Examples:
- Dimming lights 1–2 hours before bed to initiate melatonin release

- Turning off screens and stimulation at a set time

- Performing a consistent 3–5 step bedtime routine (e.g., warm shower → body oiling → breathwork → journal → sleep)

The goal is to make the transition from wakefulness to rest a *known path*, not a forced shutdown.

2. Somatic Sleep Cues

Incorporating specific **body-based cues** into the bedtime routine helps rewire threat-based associations with rest.

- **Weighted Pressure:** Using a weighted blanket or light compression wrap around the chest or hips

- **Gentle Rocking or Swaying:** Calms the vestibular system and mimics early attachment experiences

- **Humming or Toning:** Stimulates the vagus nerve and discharges sympathetic energy

- **Exhale-Extended Breathing:** 4-6-8 pattern to slow heart rate and deepen vagal tone

These cues signal to the brainstem: *You are safe. You can let go.*

3. Emotional Offloading and Cognitive Closure

The limbic system cannot rest when emotional charge is unprocessed. Bedtime rituals should create space to metabolize unresolved tension from the day.

Techniques:

- **Journal Dump:** Free-write thoughts, worries, or unfinished mental loops to clear the mind

- **Gratitude Logging:** Naming 3–5 things that went well to shift toward safety-based focus

- **Parts Check-In:** Brief internal dialogue with inner protectors or anxious parts ("Thank you, I've got it from here")

This gives the psyche closure, allowing the body to soften.

4. Multisensory Anchoring

Engage multiple senses to ground the body and prime the parasympathetic system.

- **Sound:** Soft binaural beats, ambient frequencies, or nature sounds

- **Smell:** Essential oils like lavender, clary sage, or cedarwood

- **Touch:** Silk sheets, cozy textures, or self-touch practices like hand on the heart

- **Sight:** Candlelight, darkness, or a soft night light with red hue (blue light suppresses melatonin)

This creates a sensory landscape of safety and familiarity.

5. Co-Regulation and Sleep

Many nervous systems resist sleep because they were wired for **relational hypervigilance**—especially in early environments where safety was inconsistent or absent.

When possible, rituals that include **co-regulation**—connection with another safe nervous system—can accelerate rest and downshifting.

- Lying beside a regulated partner

- Listening to a calming voice (audio recording or sleep meditation)

- Cuddling with a pet or applying gentle self-pressure as a proxy for containment

If relational safety is not accessible, **internalized co-regulation** practices (imagining a safe other, or repeating calming affirmations) can provide similar effects.

Sleep is not laziness. It is not weakness. It is **one of the deepest acts of nervous system repair**. Relearning how to rest is revolutionary—especially for bodies that have been trained to survive instead of settle. When we commit to nervous system bedtime rituals, we offer our bodies something sacred: the right to soften, to release, and to be held by the stillness we once feared.

Rest Is a Birthright, Not a Privilege

In a culture that glorifies hustle and equates exhaustion with worth, rest becomes radical. But for those with trauma histories or chronically dysregulated nervous systems, rest is more than rebellion—it is rehabilitation.

This chapter has shown that **resistance to sleep and stillness is not a personal failure**. It is a physiological imprint of past vigilance. The inability to rest is not rooted in laziness or lack of discipline; it stems from a body that was trained to survive instead of settle. Through the lens of Neurosomatic Intelligence (NSI), we see this clearly: the nervous system does not simply "turn off." It requires deliberate signaling, ritual, and safety to downshift into true parasympathetic dominance.

Tools like breath modulation, vagal toning, environmental predictability, and multisensory anchoring provide **bottom-up pathways** for nervous system recalibration. And sleep rituals, far from being luxuries, are **neurobiological invitations** for the body to repair, integrate, and recover.

Reclaiming rest is an act of profound nervous system sovereignty. It is the process of teaching the body that it no longer has to be "on." That peace is not a threat. That presence, stillness, and softness are not dangerous—but deeply restorative.

As we move into the next chapter, we will explore how **play,**

pleasure, and nervous system joy expand our capacity beyond survival. Because resilience is not just the ability to endure—it is the ability to delight, to connect, and to truly live.

References

1. **Porges SW.** The Polyvagal Theory: Neurophysiological Foundations of Emotions, Attachment, Communication, and Self-Regulation. New York, NY: W. W. Norton & Company; 2011.

2. **Walker MP.** Why We Sleep: Unlocking the Power of Sleep and Dreams. New York, NY: Scribner; 2017.

3. **Sapolsky RM.** Why Zebras Don't Get Ulcers. 3rd ed. New York, NY: Henry Holt and Company; 2004.

4. **Saper CB, Scammell TE, Lu J.** Hypothalamic regulation of sleep and circadian rhythms. Nature. 2005;437(7063):1257–1263. doi:10.1038/nature04284

5. **Craig AD.** How do you feel? Interoception: the sense of the physiological condition of the body. Nat Rev Neurosci. 2002;3(8):655–666. doi:10.1038/nrn894

6. **Owens JA, Weiss MR.** Insufficient sleep in adolescents: a perfect storm. Pediatr Clin North Am. 2017;64(4):747–764. doi:10.1016/j.pcl.2017.03.007

7. **Kahn M, Sheppes G, Sadeh A.** Sleep and emotions: Bidirectional links and underlying mechanisms. Int J Psychophysiol. 2013;89(2):218–228. doi:10.1016/j.ijpsycho.2013.05.010

8. **Goyal M, Singh S, Sibinga EMS, et al.** Meditation programs for psychological stress and well-being:

a systematic review and meta-analysis. JAMA Intern Med. 2014;174(3):357–368. doi:10.1001/jamainternmed.2013.13018

9. **Chrousos GP.** Stress and disorders of the stress system. Nat Rev Endocrinol. 2009;5(7):374–381. doi:10.1038/nrendo.2009.106

10. **Mayer EA, Labus JS, Tillisch K, Cole SW, Baldi P.** Towards a systems view of IBS. Nat Rev Gastroenterol Hepatol. 2015;12(10):592–605. doi:10.1038/nrgastro.2015.121

CHAPTER 12
Play, Joy, and Nervous System Expansion

The Biology of Joy: Why Pleasure Is a Survival Resource

Contrary to cultural conditioning that equates productivity with worthiness, joy is not a luxury—it is a biological imperative. From an evolutionary lens, the capacity to experience pleasure, curiosity, and connection is a sign of a regulated, socially engaged nervous system. These states are governed by the **ventral vagal complex**, the branch of the parasympathetic nervous system responsible for safety, bonding, and restoration (Porges, 2011).

In a dysregulated system, however, play and joy may feel inaccessible or even unsafe. Individuals who have lived in chronic survival states—such as freeze, fawn, fight, or flight—often experience positive emotions as foreign, suspicious, or fleeting. When joy does arise, it may be quickly sabotaged by guilt, hypervigilance, or self-doubt.

This phenomenon is not a character flaw. It is a learned adaptation. Neurosomatic Intelligence (NSI) views pleasure and play not as emotional indulgences but as **neural reprogramming tools**. These experiences are essential for expanding the nervous system's window of tolerance and anchoring into a post-traumatic growth paradigm.

> Joy is the body's way of saying, "I am safe enough to thrive."

In this chapter, we will explore:

- The neurophysiology of joy and social engagement

- Why play is a developmental and neurological necessity

- NSI practices that help restore access to pleasure, creativity, and spontaneous expression

- How play rewires the brain for post-traumatic growth

From Surviving to Thriving: The Neurobiology of Play and Creativity

Play is often dismissed as frivolous or juvenile, yet it is one of the most sophisticated expressions of a regulated and resilient nervous system. In childhood development, play is the foundation for learning, social bonding, emotional regulation, and adaptive flexibility. As adults, play remains equally critical—but it requires safety to emerge.

From a neuroscience perspective, play and creativity activate the **prefrontal cortex**, enhance **dopamine** release, and engage the **ventral vagal complex** (Panksepp, 1998; Porges, 2011). These systems collectively support curiosity, social connection, problem-solving, and emotional resilience. Play allows the nervous system to experiment with novelty and uncertainty in a low-stakes context, strengthening the capacity for adaptive responses under pressure.

In trauma-impacted individuals, the brain is often dominated by **limbic survival circuits**—geared toward danger detection and rapid response. In such states, creativity shuts down. Imagination becomes restricted to anticipating threat. Joy and spontaneity are perceived as risky. This is why survivors often feel "serious," "stuck," or "cut off" from their playful selves.

Neurosomatic Intelligence reframes this loss of playfulness as a **neuroprotective adaptation**. The nervous system has not failed—it has been protecting you. But now, as regulation returns, so can pleasure. By slowly reintroducing play into daily life, we send powerful signals to the body and brain: "It is safe to be here. It is safe to explore. It is safe to feel good."

Signs That the Nervous System Is Ready to Play:

- You begin to feel curious again, rather than just cautious

- Laughter arises spontaneously

- You feel less need to control outcomes and more freedom to explore

- Movement feels expressive, not obligatory

- You tolerate "not knowing" without panic

These moments may be small, but they represent monumental shifts in neurobiology—from survival to expansion, from contraction to coherence.

> Creativity is not a luxury—it is a sign that the nervous system is healing.

NSI Practices to Restore Joy, Play, and Pleasure

In the Neurosomatic Intelligence (NSI) framework, play is not just a behavior—it's a **nervous system capacity**. Just as we train regulation, we must also train joy. These practices aren't about forcing happiness; they're about gradually inviting aliveness back into the system.

Reclaiming play and pleasure is a **bottom-up process**—meaning we engage the body first, not the intellect. These NSI practices help reopen the circuits of curiosity, delight, and creativity, even for those whose trauma histories have dulled their capacity to feel joy.

Embodied Joy Practices

1. **Spontaneous Movement Exploration**

    - Set a timer for 3–5 minutes. Let the body move however it wants—silly, slow, big, small. Don't choreograph. Follow sensation.

    - This builds tolerance for non-linear movement and uncovers new "safe" somatic pathways.

2. **Vocal Play**

    - Make unusual sounds: hums, whooshes, growls, song fragments. Play with pitch and rhythm.

    - Stimulates the ventral vagus nerve and rewires vocal inhibition from early relational wounds.

3. **Mirroring Games** (Solo or with a partner)

    - Copy the movements of a partner (or your reflection) with exaggerated expression. This co-regulates and builds relational safety.

4. **Object Curiosity**

    - Choose a random object. Explore it with wonder—how it feels, smells, sounds. This builds novelty-tolerance and sensory pleasure.

Pleasure and Sensory Reconnection

Many survivors have an aversive or numb relationship with pleasure. These practices gently reawaken the body's ability to receive and enjoy sensory input:

- **Tactile Luxuries:** Rubbing soft textures on your skin, wearing cozy socks, or taking warm baths.

- **Taste Rituals:** Eating one bite of food slowly, exploring flavor and texture with mindfulness.

- **Nature Play:** Barefoot walks on grass, watching clouds, climbing a tree—rebuilding wonder through safe environmental interaction.

These activities help reclaim the body as a **source of delight**, not just danger.

Neuroplasticity Through Joy

Repeated safe experiences of play and pleasure **rewire the brain**. Each time the nervous system engages in a joyful act without consequence, it updates the internal model: *Not everything leads to danger. Feeling good is safe.*

In NSI, we view play and pleasure as **regulatory anchors**—tools to create new neural templates for embodiment, self-expression, and connection.

> "Joy is not a distraction from healing. Joy is a nervous system intervention."

Shame, Suppression, and the Cultural Cost of Joylessness

In many cultures and communities, joy is not merely absent—it has been suppressed, shamed, or sacrificed for survival. For those navigating systems of oppression, historical trauma, or inherited struggle, playfulness is often labeled as childish, irresponsible, or even dangerous. Joy becomes a privilege rather than a right.

The Nervous System Cost of Joy Suppression

When joy is repressed, the nervous system loses access to

ventral vagal states—those rooted in connection, creativity, and calm. Without these states, individuals live in chronic mobilization (fight/flight) or immobilization (freeze/shutdown), unable to experience ease, spontaneity, or pleasure.

Cultural messages such as:

- "Don't laugh too loud."
- "Stay vigilant."
- "Work first, rest later."
- "You're too much."

...embed themselves in the body as cues of danger. Over time, this erodes a person's **capacity to receive**, express, or even trust moments of joy. Especially in BIPOC, LGBTQ+, neurodivergent, and immigrant communities, the policing of expression becomes internalized as a survival reflex.

Intergenerational Echoes of Joylessness

When joy is absent across generations, it doesn't simply disappear—it becomes woven into the fabric of family systems and cultural identity. It gets encoded in expectations, rules, and nervous system responses. The message passed down—often without words—is that joy is unsafe, unearned, or irrelevant when survival is at stake.

The Inheritance of Emotional Survivalism

In many trauma-impacted families, joy is sacrificed for vigilance. Hyper-responsibility becomes a badge of honor. Stillness becomes laziness. Emotional suppression is mistaken for maturity. Laughter feels like a betrayal to the pain that came before.

Children growing up in these environments

internalize the unspoken codes:

- *"Stay quiet, stay safe."*
- *"Don't celebrate too loud, something bad always follows."*
- *"We don't have time for play—we have work to do."*

As a result, joy becomes foreign—an emotion experienced with guilt or hesitation. Not because families didn't love—but because they were surviving.

Nervous System Imprints

Neurosomatic Intelligence (NSI) teaches that the nervous system learns through experience and repetition. When joy is absent or punished across generations, the brain and body stop recognizing it as a safe state. Even in adulthood, attempts to feel good may activate alarm bells in the form of:

- Self-sabotage after success
- Guilt after moments of pleasure
- Shame when being seen or celebrated
- Physical discomfort with rest or praise

This is not a mindset issue—it is an intergenerational nervous system imprint.

Reclaiming Joy as Somatic Medicine

But what if joy isn't indulgent or naive? What if it is medicine—biological *and* spiritual? In NSI, we frame joy as a **regenerative force**. It repairs, restores, and expands the window of tolerance. It invites the ventral vagal system—the seat of connection, creativity, and calm—back online.

To reclaim joy is not to deny past pain, but to interrupt the belief that joy must always be earned, postponed, or feared. It is to say:

- *"I am allowed to feel good, even if they couldn't."*
- *"I can honor their survival and choose something more."*
- *"My nervous system is safe enough now to feel joy without bracing for the fall."*

Cultural and Familial Alchemy

This reclamation isn't just personal—it is ancestral alchemy. Every moment of laughter, play, and pleasure becomes a declaration that the lineage of emotional suppression ends here. It sends new signals up and down the nervous system ladder, informing future generations that joy is not a threat—it's home.

Joy, in this way, becomes an act of resistance. A reclamation. A radical rewiring of what our bodies, families, and communities are allowed to feel.

Somatic Shame and Play Inhibition

Shame is not just an emotion—it is a full-body state of contraction, inhibition, and perceived disconnection from safety or worth. It is one of the most potent inhibitors of joy and play, particularly in individuals with trauma, chronic dysregulation, or identity-based marginalization.

Unlike guilt, which says *"I did something wrong,"* shame whispers (or shouts), *"I **am** something wrong."* This core belief hijacks the nervous system and limits access to spontaneous expression, creativity, and pleasure.

The Physiology of Shame

From a Neurosomatic Intelligence (NSI) lens, shame manifests as a **polyvagal shutdown**—a dorsal vagal state characterized by immobilization, dissociation, and emotional suppression. In this state, the body protects itself by becoming small, invisible, or silent. These physiological cues often appear as:

- **Collapsed posture**: Hunched shoulders, downcast head, tension in the throat or chest

- **Avoidant eye contact**: Difficulty maintaining connection, hyper-awareness of gaze

- **Suppressed laughter or movement**: Fear of being "too much," "too loud," or "childish"

- **Hyper-self-monitoring**: Overanalyzing behavior, fearing judgment, masking natural impulses

Shame creates a chronic "freeze" loop around expression. It teaches the body that being seen is dangerous. That joy is unsafe. That play is for those who haven't been hurt.

Why Shame Blocks Play

Play requires **vulnerability**. It asks us to take risks, be silly, make mistakes, and move without purpose. In contrast, shame creates rigidity—an inner demand for perfection, control, and approval. When these two states collide, the nervous system prioritizes self-protection over self-expression.

Children who were mocked, shamed, or punished for being expressive often grow into adults who:

- Fear public embarrassment or failure

- Avoid dancing, singing, or spontaneous movement

- Struggle to relax in social settings

- Feel uncomfortable when others are playful or carefree

This isn't immaturity—it's embodied inhibition rooted in survival adaptation.

Rewiring Through Micro-Play and Safety

NSI practitioners understand that you can't "think" your way out of shame—you must **move** through it. Not by forcing joy, but by **inviting small, safe experiments** in embodiment.

We begin with **micro-play**:

- Making silly faces in the mirror
- Wiggling fingers to music
- Whispering spontaneous sounds
- Trying out a silly walk in private
- Using breath and laughter in short bursts

These are not childish—they are **neurological interventions**. They help reclaim access to ventral vagal states by slowly building tolerance for visibility, novelty, and expression.

In safe relational containers, these micro-movements interrupt the shame loop and offer new outcomes: *You were playful, and nothing bad happened.* Over time, the body begins to trust that lightness does not equal danger.

Reclaiming the Right to Be Seen and Silly

Healing shame is not about performing confidence—it is about creating nervous system conditions that allow **authenticity without collapse**. When shame is metabolized somatically, individuals begin to:

- Laugh more freely

- Move without self-judgment

- Express desires, preferences, and creativity

- Enjoy being seen and celebrated

The capacity for joy, play, and pleasure becomes possible not because shame is gone—but because the nervous system no longer needs it as protection.

In this way, joy becomes a **form of somatic freedom** —the ability to be who you are, without armor. And play becomes a portal back to the self that was never broken, only buried under the weight of shame.

Healing Joylessness Through Embodied Joy

Joy is not a frivolous bonus in the human experience—it is a **biological necessity**. From a Neurosomatic Intelligence (NSI) perspective, joy is not just an emotion; it is a **neurophysiological state of safety**, connection, and regulation. It signals that the nervous system is not in survival mode. It confirms that we are safe enough to expand, create, and connect.

However, for many, the ability to feel joy has been eroded by trauma, oppression, over-responsibility, and a cultural overemphasis on productivity and stoicism. The result is a chronic state of **joylessness**—a condition in which pleasure, play, and lightness feel foreign, indulgent, or even dangerous.

The Nervous System Cost of Joylessness

When joy is chronically absent, the nervous system adapts by shrinking the **window of tolerance**. This means that anything outside of hypervigilance or overachievement feels unsafe. Over time, even rest, laughter, or softness can trigger discomfort.

Joylessness is not laziness, apathy, or weakness. It is a **protective adaptation**—a survival-based way of living that deprioritizes aliveness in favor of vigilance, performance, or obedience.

This is especially true in individuals who have lived in systems or cultures where joy was viewed as:

- Distracting or irresponsible

- Undeserved or selfish

- Threatening to authority

- A luxury rather than a right

Such conditioning creates **emotional scarcity**—a belief that joy is for "later," "better people," or "more stable times." But in NSI, we challenge this myth. Joy is not earned—it is *reclaimed*.

Reintroducing Joy Through the Body

To restore joy, we must go *through* the body—not around it. NSI practitioners use **embodied joy practices** that gently rebuild a person's capacity to feel and express positive states. These might include:

- **Movement play**: Dancing, swaying, bouncing, or shaking to upbeat music

- **Vocal exploration**: Singing, humming, chanting, or laughing with intention

- **Sensory delight**: Engaging textures, smells, tastes, or sounds that spark pleasure

- **Facial expression**: Smiling, widening the eyes, or softening the face to activate the social engagement system

- **Mirror work**: Making silly faces or practicing affirmations with embodied posture

These aren't just feel-good activities—they are **neurological retraining tools**. Each playful act signals to the brain: *The threat is gone. It is safe to feel joy again.*

Even just a few seconds of embodied joy per day can shift nervous system patterns, especially when practiced with intention and repetition. Over time, these micro-moments of pleasure coalesce into a **resilient internal baseline**—one where joy is no longer foreign, but familiar.

The Collective Impact of Reclaimed Joy

The cultural cost of joylessness is steep. When communities are robbed of joy, they are robbed of innovation, hope, and cohesion. Without joy, burnout festers, relationships fracture, and resistance becomes harder to sustain.

But joy is **contagious**. One person reclaiming joy sends ripples through families, workplaces, and entire communities. It softens hardened systems. It invites others to exhale. It reminds people that life is not just about surviving—but *thriving*.

To reclaim joy is to challenge trauma, capitalism, white supremacy, and shame at the somatic level. It is a radical act of **embodied rebellion**—a declaration that you are more than your wounds. That you are here not just to endure, but to **feel**, to **laugh**, to **love**, and to **create**.

> "To play is to declare: *I am safe. I belong. I exist beyond survival.*"

In reclaiming joy, we return to ourselves—not as broken beings, but as whole humans with the capacity for deep pleasure, purpose, and connection.

Clinical Vignette: Reclaiming Joy After Burnout

Client: "Aaliyah", 38, Black woman, social worker

Presenting Issue: Chronic fatigue, emotional numbness, guilt around pleasure, history of trauma and hyper-independence

Case Overview:

Aaliyah entered therapy reporting that she felt "robotic," "exhausted," and "disconnected from everything I used to love." Despite serving her community tirelessly for over a decade, she hadn't laughed or danced in years. Her life revolved around caregiving, deadlines, and managing crises—for others. When asked about her relationship with joy, Aaliyah paused and said, *"That's for other people. I don't have time for joy."*

She also shared that growing up, expressions of happiness were rare. Her mother, a single parent and trauma survivor, often said, *"We don't have time to play—we have to survive."* Laughter was punished, softness was dismissed, and silence was often the safest choice.

NSI-Based Intervention:

Using NSI protocols, we began with **foundational safety drills** to downshift her hyperaroused nervous system—extended exhales, orienting, and co-regulation techniques. As regulation increased, Aaliyah was invited to experiment with **micro-moments of embodied joy**:

- In session, she practiced **swaying slowly** to music she used to enjoy in her teens.

- She incorporated **mirror play**—smiling at herself in the mirror and saying affirmations.

- She began a "30 seconds of joy" practice—choosing one playful or pleasurable act each day: walking barefoot in grass, doodling, or dancing in her kitchen.

At first, these acts triggered shame. She would laugh and then instantly tense. We explored this response through **somatic tracking**, uncovering intergenerational messages that joy was dangerous or wasteful. Through gentle, repeated exposure and nervous system regulation, that shame began to melt.

Outcome:
Over several months, Aaliyah began to reclaim her **embodied right to joy**. She joined a weekly dance class. She laughed freely again. Her posture softened. She no longer saw joy as a threat, but as a resource.

> "For the first time in my life," she said, "I'm learning how to feel good without guilt."

Clinician Note:

Aaliyah's case highlights the **intergenerational inhibition of joy** and how nervous system-based practices can restore access to positive affective states. Her healing journey underscores that joy isn't a byproduct of healing—it's a **critical input**. NSI offers a structure where joy is not only permitted but prescribed as somatic medicine.

Reclaiming Joy as a Somatic Birthright

Play is not childish. Joy is not frivolous. These states are essential markers of a nervous system that feels safe, alive, and connected. When we reclaim play, laughter, curiosity, and pleasure, we are not abandoning responsibility—we are completing the trauma cycle and stepping into a fuller, freer expression of life.

In a world conditioned by hustle, trauma, and generational hypervigilance, joy often feels like a distant memory or a guilty indulgence. But Neurosomatic Intelligence (NSI) reminds us: **joy is a state of regulation**. It is what emerges when the body no longer needs to defend, perform, or collapse.

Throughout this chapter, we've explored how play and creativity are not luxuries but necessities—neurobiologically linked to emotional resilience, cognitive flexibility, and social bonding. We've also confronted the deep cultural and intergenerational costs of joylessness, especially within marginalized communities, where pleasure has often been pathologized or policed.

Now, we invite you to imagine a new nervous system story. One where rest is honored. Where movement is expressive. Where your laughter echoes louder than your fear. Where joy is not an afterthought—it is a **reclamation**.

You are not too much. You are not broken. You are wired for joy.

And every time you play, dance, sing, or express yourself without apology—you're not just healing yourself. You're rewriting what safety looks and feels like for every generation to come.

References

- **Brown, B. (2012).** *Daring Greatly: How the Courage to Be Vulnerable Transforms the Way We Live, Love, Parent, and Lead.* Gotham Books.

- **Cozolino, L. (2014).** *The Neuroscience of Human Relationships: Attachment and the Developing Social Brain* (2nd ed.). W. W. Norton & Company.

- **Porges, S. W. (2011).** *The Polyvagal Theory: Neurophysiological Foundations of Emotions, Attachment, Communication, and Self-regulation.* W. W. Norton & Company.

- **Schore, A. N. (2012).** *The Science of the Art of Psychotherapy.* W. W. Norton & Company.

- **Siegel, D. J. (2010).** *The Mindful Therapist: A Clinician's Guide to Mindsight and Neural Integration.* W. W. Norton & Company.

- **Stuart, A. & Noyes, M. (2021).** "The Neurobiology of Play: Linking Early Childhood Exploration to Later Life Creativity and Regulation." *Developmental Psychology Review,* 37(3), 148–164. https://doi.org/10.1016/j.dr.2021.01.003

- **Trevarthen, C. (2009).** "The Interpersonal Foundations of Human Consciousness." In *Neurobiology of Human Values,* ed. Jean-Pierre Changeux et al. Springer.

- **van der Kolk, B. A. (2014).** *The Body Keeps the Score: Brain, Mind, and Body in the Healing of Trauma.* Viking.

- **Winnicott, D. W. (1971).** *Playing and Reality.* Tavistock Publications.

SECTION IV: INTEGRATION AND TRANSFORMATION

CHAPTER 13
Inner Critic, Shame & Self-Compassion

When Shame Speaks Louder Than Self

Shame is not just a passing emotion—it is a full-body shutdown. It is the felt sense that "something is wrong with me," not because of what we've done, but because of who we are. It constricts breath, drops eye gaze, collapses posture, and often silences the voice. When shame is chronic or internalized, it becomes an invisible cage that dictates our choices, relationships, and ability to self-regulate.

For many, the *inner critic*—that relentless voice of judgment—originates not in character defect but in early relational trauma. It echoes the unmet expectations, criticisms, or emotional withholding experienced in formative environments. Over time, this internal monologue becomes reflexive: "I'm too much." "I'm not enough." "I shouldn't feel this." "I'll never get it right."

From a **Neurosomatic Intelligence (NSI)** lens, shame is not viewed as a failing of the self—it is a *nervous system strategy* for safety. If the child learned that expressing anger led to punishment, that asking for help resulted in neglect, or that making a mistake brought ridicule, the nervous system adapted by shrinking, hiding, and silencing. In this way, shame becomes a **neurobiological shield**—an attempt to avoid further harm through self-inhibition.

This physiological imprint of shame often results in:

- **Dorsal vagal dominance** (freeze, collapse, and

disconnection)

- **Suppressed self-expression** (difficulty setting boundaries or speaking needs)

- **Inflammatory responses** (linked to chronic illness and autoimmune activation)

- **Hypervigilance around performance and approval**

Crucially, the problem is not that shame exists—but that it goes unchallenged and unprocessed. NSI invites us to interrupt the shame loop not with logic or force, but with **somatic compassion**—a bottom-up, body-first approach to restoring dignity and safety in the self. This includes practices like gentle touch, breath-based self-soothing, and co-regulated presence with trusted others.

Shame is not an enemy to be defeated—it is a signal to be understood. It marks the places where we were once silenced, rejected, or unseen. And it offers an invitation: to turn toward the parts of ourselves we've hidden, and meet them not with judgment, but with gentleness.

In the pages that follow, we will explore:

- The neurobiology of shame and its link to systemic inflammation

- The limitations of cognitive self-help in addressing deep-rooted shame

- Somatic tools that rewire the inner critic and awaken embodied compassion

Because when we begin to feel safe inside our own skin, the voice of shame no longer drowns out the truth of who we are.

And that is the moment self-healing begins.

The Neurology of Shame and Inflammation

Shame is not just psychological—it is profoundly biological. It affects the entire nervous system, endocrine system, and immune system. Repeated experiences of shame—especially in early development—can imprint deeply into the body, becoming a chronic stressor that alters the brain's wiring and the body's internal chemistry.

From a **neurosomatic perspective**, shame activates the **dorsal vagal branch** of the parasympathetic nervous system, leading to a shutdown or freeze state. This is experienced as collapse, fogginess, low energy, disconnection, and numbness. Rather than energizing action (as guilt or anger might), shame pulls us inward and downward, disrupting our capacity to connect, speak, and self-regulate.

Neuroimaging studies have shown that shame activates key regions of the brain associated with pain and self-monitoring, including:

- The **insula**, responsible for internal state awareness (interoception)

- The **anterior cingulate cortex**, associated with social pain and self-judgment

- The **amygdala**, triggering fear and hypervigilance

- The **default mode network (DMN)**, involved in internal narrative and rumination

These neurological activations explain why shame feels so visceral and paralyzing. It's not just "in your head"—it is in your entire system.

Shame and Inflammation

Research also shows a compelling link between shame and **chronic inflammation**. Long-term self-criticism and suppressed emotional expression correlate with elevated levels of **pro-inflammatory cytokines**, such as **IL-6**, **TNF-alpha**, and **CRP** (C-reactive protein). These inflammatory markers have been associated with:

- Autoimmune conditions
- Cardiovascular disease
- Depression and anxiety
- Gastrointestinal disorders (via the gut-brain axis)

According to **Sapolsky (2004)** and others in the field of stress research, emotional repression and social isolation—common consequences of chronic shame—may provoke a prolonged activation of the **hypothalamic-pituitary-adrenal (HPA) axis**, keeping cortisol levels elevated and increasing vulnerability to disease.

This suggests that shame is not only emotionally distressing—it is biologically toxic. When shame becomes a trait rather than a state (i.e., chronic rather than situational), it shapes our posture, our perception of the world, our immunity, and even our gene expression.

Reframing Shame as Adaptive

In NSI, shame is not framed as weakness or failure, but as an **intelligent adaptation**—a neuroprotective reflex to maintain attachment and survival. Especially in childhood, where dependency is high and autonomy is low, shame serves as an internal leash: "If I self-correct before they correct me, maybe I can stay safe." This internalized correction becomes the seed of the inner critic.

But what was once protective becomes limiting when it remains unchecked in adulthood. The nervous system continues to police our authenticity long after the original threat is gone. The result is a life lived through inhibition, self-censorship, and emotional isolation.

By recognizing the **neurological and physiological roots of shame**, we can move beyond blame and into healing. With gentle, body-first practices, we begin to soften the shame response—not by denying it, but by offering the system a new experience of safety, connection, and worthiness.

The Power of Non-Cognitive Interventions

Traditional models of healing shame often rely on cognitive reframing, affirmations, or talk therapy. While these approaches can be helpful, they often fall short when the shame is somatically embedded. The inner critic does not live solely in the logical brain—it lives in the body, the breath, the posture, and the reflexes of self-protection.

This is where **Neurosomatic Intelligence (NSI)** provides a powerful alternative: healing shame through **bottom-up interventions** that work directly with the nervous system.

Why Thinking Isn't Enough

Shame arises from early relational wounds, often before we had language. These experiences bypass the prefrontal cortex and get stored in **subcortical** and **limbic regions** of the brain—areas that are not easily accessed through reasoning or insight alone. As **Levine (1997)** and **van der Kolk (2014)** describe, trauma and shame live in the body, and therefore, must be addressed through the body.

When clients are told to "just think positive" or "love

yourself more," they may feel further invalidated or even retraumatized. They understand the concept of self-love, but their body doesn't feel safe enough to receive it. The shame response is not a logic problem—it is a **state problem**.

NSI respects the reality that **state creates story**. To change the internal narrative, we must first shift the physiological state.

Somatic Interventions That Interrupt Shame

1. **Vocal Vagal Toning**
   Humming, chanting, or singing stimulates the **ventral vagus nerve**, activating the social engagement system and reducing shame-induced collapse. It also invites vocal expression, which is often suppressed in shame states.

2. **Postural Repatterning**
   Shame lives in a collapsed posture—rounded shoulders, bowed head, downcast eyes. Practicing upright, expansive posture (with gentleness, not force) sends new signals to the brain: *I am allowed to take up space.*

3. **Breath Regulation**
   Shame constricts breath. Practices like **extended exhale breathing** or **sighing** help release tension from the diaphragm and increase vagal tone, making it easier to shift out of immobilization.

4. **Self-Contact and Tactile Soothing**
   Placing a hand on the heart, cheek, or solar plexus can co-regulate the nervous system. Safe, gentle touch activates **C-tactile afferents**, signaling safety and emotional warmth to the brainstem.

5. **Eye Gaze Practice**

Practicing safe eye contact (even with a mirror or trusted practitioner) helps repair ruptures in the **social engagement system**, where much of the original shame was encoded.

6. **Playful Movement and Micro-Expressions**
Shame often inhibits spontaneity. Encouraging subtle movements like eyebrow lifts, shoulder rolls, or silly faces creates micro-disruptions in the shame loop and opens access to joy, curiosity, and relational engagement.

Co-Regulation as a Catalyst

One of the most potent non-cognitive interventions is **co-regulation**—the experience of being in the presence of a calm, attuned, regulated nervous system. For many, shame was born in relationships where vulnerability was met with criticism or neglect. Healing must happen in relationships where vulnerability is met with **presence and permission**.

NSI practitioners use **attuned presence** to create a neuroceptive environment of safety, allowing clients to experience acceptance at the level of the body. This is not about fixing or analyzing—it's about being with. When the body learns that it can be seen, felt, and held without shame, a new story becomes possible.

Cultivating Somatic Compassion

Self-compassion is not merely a mindset—it is a **felt sense of inner safety and permission**. For individuals living with chronic shame or self-criticism, the concept of compassion often feels abstract or inaccessible. In *Neurosomatic Intelligence (NSI)*, compassion is cultivated not just through thought, but through **body-based practices** that restore safety, connection, and internal kindness.

What Is Somatic Compassion?

Somatic compassion is the practice of bringing kindness, curiosity, and nonjudgmental presence to our internal experience. It is how we **respond to our own dysregulation**, distress, or discomfort without collapsing into shame or spiraling into self-abandonment.

In nervous system terms, somatic compassion means building the **capacity to stay present** with uncomfortable sensations—tightness, heat, tremors, numbness—while **remaining regulated** and **resourced**.

It is not about "fixing" the feeling. It is about creating the conditions in which the nervous system feels safe enough to unfold, express, and complete.

> "You cannot hate yourself into healing. But you can *feel* yourself into wholeness."

Practices to Build Somatic Compassion

1. **Pendulation Between Safety and Discomfort**
   Borrowed from Somatic Experiencing (Levine, 1997), pendulation is the practice of shifting attention between a resource (a part of the body that feels neutral or pleasant) and a place of discomfort. This teaches the body that pain is not totalizing—and that safety can coexist with challenge.

2. **Name and Normalize**
   Instead of labeling your sensations as "bad" or "too much," try naming them neutrally: "There is heat in my chest," "I feel pressure in my shoulders," "My jaw is tight." Then affirm: *Of course this is here. It makes sense that my body remembers.* This reduces inner resistance and invites softening.

3. **Compassionate Self-Touch**
   Gently holding or stroking the part of your body experiencing discomfort communicates care and containment. Wrapping arms around your torso or placing a hand over your heart activates oxytocin release and reduces sympathetic arousal.

4. **Internal Dialogue in a Soothing Tone**
   Shame often speaks in harsh, parental tones. Try speaking to yourself as you would to a child or beloved friend. Say out loud: "It's okay to feel this. You're doing your best. I'm here with you." Tone of voice matters—it calms the limbic system and restores emotional safety.

5. **Mirror Work and Affirmation with Gaze**
   Looking into your own eyes and offering affirmation (e.g., "You are enough," "You are safe now," "You didn't deserve that") can repattern old imprints of shame and abandonment. Pairing this with breathwork or gentle movement increases its somatic impact.

Compassion is a Muscle—Not a Mood

Just like physical strength, somatic compassion is a capacity that builds through repetition and care. In the beginning, it may feel awkward or even triggering to offer kindness to yourself—but that discomfort is a sign that the nervous system is learning something new.

As NSI teaches, **healing is not about erasing the past**—it's about creating **new patterns in the present**. When you meet yourself with gentleness, even in small doses, your nervous system rewires toward safety, resilience, and dignity.

With time, the inner critic loses its grip. Not because it was banished, but because it was **seen, soothed, and softened** by a wiser, more loving inner presence.

From Criticism to Compassion

Shame is not a flaw of character—it is a strategy of survival. It is how the nervous system attempts to maintain safety in the face of relational threat, unmet needs, or abandonment. The inner critic is not our enemy; it is the echo of past pain trying to protect us from future harm.

But protection is not the same as liberation.

Through the lens of Neurosomatic Intelligence, we reframe shame not as pathology, but as physiology. We learn that chronic self-criticism is not simply negative thinking—it is a pattern of dysregulation stored in the body, one that constricts breath, posture, voice, and vitality. Left unaddressed, this pattern reinforces cycles of inflammation, disconnection, and emotional suppression.

And yet, we are not bound to this legacy.

Self-compassion is not a luxury. It is a biological intervention. When we offer kindness to ourselves through tone, touch, breath, and presence, we activate the very systems responsible for healing, immunity, and connection. Somatic compassion—gentle, grounded, embodied—becomes the practice through which we reparent our nervous system and reclaim our internal landscape from the grip of shame.

The journey from shame to safety is not about becoming someone new. It is about **returning to who we were before the world told us we were too much, too sensitive, too wrong.**

You were never too much. Your emotions were never the

problem. Your body was never the enemy. What you needed—what we all need—is to be met with presence, with protection, and with love.

In the chapters ahead, we will explore the final pieces of the nervous system's return to wholeness: grief, identity, integration, and legacy. Because the goal is not just regulation—it is reclamation. The body is not just meant to survive trauma—it is meant to **thrive in truth**.
Let your healing be your homecoming.

References

Craig, A. D. (2002). How do you feel? Interoception: the sense of the physiological condition of the body. *Nature Reviews Neuroscience*, 3(8), 655–666. https://doi.org/10.1038/nrn894

Gilbert, P. (2009). *The Compassionate Mind: A New Approach to Life's Challenges*. New Harbinger Publications.

Kemeny, M. E., Gruenewald, T. L., & Dickerson, S. S. (2004). Shame as the emotional response to threat to the social self: Implications for behavior, physiology, and health. *Psychological Inquiry*, 15(2), 153–160. https://doi.org/10.1207/s15327965pli1502_03

Lanius, R. A., Paulsen, S., & Corrigan, F. (2014). *Neurobiology and Treatment of Traumatic Dissociation: Toward an Embodied Self*. Springer Publishing Company.

Neff, K. D. (2011). *Self-compassion: The Proven Power of Being Kind to Yourself*. William Morrow.

Porges, S. W. (2011). *The Polyvagal Theory: Neurophysiological Foundations of Emotions, Attachment, Communication, and Self-Regulation*. W. W. Norton & Company.

Sapolsky, R. M. (2004). *Why Zebras Don't Get Ulcers* (3rd ed.). Henry Holt and Company.

Siegel, D. J. (2012). *The Developing Mind: How Relationships and the Brain Interact to Shape Who We Are* (2nd ed.). The Guilford Press.

Tracy, J. L., & Robins, R. W. (2004). Putting the self into self-conscious emotions: A theoretical model. *Psychological Inquiry*, 15(2), 103–125. https://doi.org/10.1207/s15327965pli1502_01

Van der Kolk, B. A. (2014). *The Body Keeps the Score: Brain, Mind, and Body in the Healing of Trauma.* Viking.

CHAPTER 14
Grief, Identity, and Integration

The Sacred Process of Grief

Grief is often misunderstood as a linear emotional state with predictable stages. In truth, grief is a **neurobiological recalibration**—a full-body, full-soul process that arises when we lose someone or something that anchored our nervous system to a sense of safety, meaning, or identity.

From a Neurosomatic Intelligence (NSI) perspective, grief is not just emotional pain—it is the body's way of reorganizing itself after loss. Whether the loss is a loved one, a relationship, a role, a community, or even a version of self, grief activates survival circuitry, disrupts routine neurochemistry, and plunges the nervous system into profound dysregulation.

Physiological symptoms may include:

- Dysregulated sleep patterns
- Appetite changes
- Chest tightness or breath constriction
- Fatigue, brain fog, and cognitive dulling

Grief, like trauma, lives in the body. But unlike trauma, which stems from threat, grief arises from **love, meaning, and connection**. It is the body's protest to the void left behind.

In NSI, we do not pathologize grief—we honor it. We create space for its waves. We learn to breathe alongside it instead of bracing against it. And we recognize that grief is not something to "get over," but something to be **integrated** as part of a whole, evolving identity.

Grief and the Reformation of Identity

Loss destabilizes identity. We must not only grieve what was lost—we must also grieve who we were in relationship to what was lost. Whether we are mourning the end of a role (such as parent, partner, or caregiver) or the loss of a dream, grief shakes the foundation of how we see ourselves.

This loss of identity can trigger survival responses:

- **Collapse** ("I don't know who I am anymore")
- **Fight** ("I have to prove I'm still worthy")
- **Flight** ("I'll avoid the pain by staying busy")
- **Fawn** ("I'll adopt others' identities to stay connected")

NSI teaches that identity is not static—it is somatic. As our nervous system recalibrates, so too does our sense of self. Grief becomes the compost through which a new, more rooted identity can emerge.

This process may feel disorienting. Old roles no longer fit. Familiar rhythms fall away. But through nervous system safety, we gain the capacity to explore new edges of identity without abandoning the core of who we are. The reformation of identity after grief requires **space**, **slowness**, and **somatic anchoring**. It is not a sprint toward reinvention, but a return to integrity—one breath, one tremble, one truth at a time.

Somatic Practices for Integrating Grief

Grief integration involves allowing the body to complete emotional and physiological loops left incomplete by sudden or unresolved loss. This means we don't just talk about grief—we **feel it**, **express it**, and **honor it** in ways that the nervous system can metabolize.

Practices include:

- **Grief Tremoring:** Gentle, rhythmic shaking to discharge held tension and reduce sympathetic dominance
- **Breath and Sounding:** Long, extended exhales paired with vocal expressions such as sighs, keens, moans, or hums to regulate vagal tone and discharge emotional intensity
- **Grief Altars or Ritual Spaces:** Creating visual and sacred containers that allow the body to anchor in symbolic safety while honoring memory, loss, and lineage
- **Embodied Storytelling:** Sharing the narrative of loss through movement, gesture, tone, and posture—allowing nonverbal processing to occur alongside cognitive reflection
- **Nature Co-Regulation:** Using the regulation of the natural world (trees, water, sun, soil) to settle the system and allow the emotional charge to be held and witnessed by something larger than self.

These practices provide pathways for the nervous system to exit survival states and enter parasympathetic integration. By creating a somatic vocabulary for grief, we invite coherence, movement, and meaning—not by bypassing grief, but by metabolizing it through felt safety and embodied honoring.

The Bridge Between Pain and Purpose

Grief, when honored through the body, becomes more than a process of mourning—it becomes a portal for redefinition. While it does not erase pain or undo loss, it holds the potential to deepen one's relationship with self, others, and life itself. From a Neurosomatic Intelligence (NSI) perspective, this integration represents the shift from dysregulation to depth, from fragmentation to coherence.

Grief softens the egoic structure, humbles the nervous system, and awakens what has long been dormant: empathy, attunement, and embodied truth. The body, when allowed to tremble, cry, collapse, or rise with the wave of grief, begins to reorganize its neural patterns. What was once braced against life becomes available for it. Through that reclamation, purpose does not override pain—it emerges beside it, rooted in lived experience and emotional truth.

This transformation is not linear. It is cyclical and somatic. A person may find themselves returning to the same grief again and again, but each time with more capacity, more embodiment, and more clarity. Over time, the story of grief no longer ends with loss—it expands into legacy.

NSI practitioners often observe that clients who engage in embodied grief rituals begin to access a different quality of presence: they become more relational, more grounded, and more aligned with a sense of "why" that feels internally sourced rather than externally imposed. This is not performance-based resilience; it is authentic post-traumatic growth—earned through emotional integrity and nervous system coherence.

Grief becomes the soil in which purpose takes root. And that purpose, born not from bypass but from brave embodiment, becomes medicine not only for the individual, but for the collective. Through our capacity to grieve, we reclaim our capacity to serve, love, and lead—fully alive, fully human.

Grief is not something we move past—it is something we move with. In the Neurosomatic Intelligence model, grief is understood not as an emotional inconvenience to be silenced, but as a sacred intelligence of the body asking to be felt, witnessed, and honored.

We grieve because we have loved. And in the wake of loss, the nervous system must renegotiate its sense of safety, connection, and identity. This chapter has explored how somatic practices can support this reorganization—not to fix what was lost, but to integrate its imprint into a new, expanded sense of self.

When grief is metabolized rather than suppressed, it becomes generative. It can birth clarity, soften judgment, deepen presence, and anchor a more rooted sense of purpose. Through tremoring, sounding, storytelling, and ritual, we give the body permission to alchemize sorrow into strength, longing into love, and loss into legacy.

Your grief is not a weakness. It is wisdom, expressed through sensation. And when held with reverence, it becomes one of the most profound portals to healing and wholeness.

Practitioner Tools: Supporting Clients Through Somatic Grief Integration

1. Grief Mapping Exercise
Purpose: Help clients locate where grief is stored or felt in the body
Instructions:
- Ask the client to close their eyes and name the first part of the body that "feels heavy" when they think about the loss.

- Invite gentle touch or breath directed toward that area.

- Have them name any sensations (tightness, pulsing, dullness) and any associated images or memories.

- Let them draw or journal the map as a visual representation of where grief is held.

2. Anchor Object Ritual
Purpose: Provide sensory anchoring and symbolic continuity
Instructions:
- Invite the client to choose a small object that reminds

them of the person, role, or experience they've lost.

- Encourage them to carry or place it in a visible area.

- Use the object as a somatic anchor during sessions—clients can hold it when grief arises, allowing a felt sense of presence and continuity.

3. Reclamation Timeline
Purpose: Support identity reconstruction post-loss
Instructions:
- Guide the client in creating a three-part timeline:
    - Who I Was Before
    - What Grief Changed
    - Who I Am Becoming

- Use somatic prompts for each section (e.g., "When you say this out loud, what do you feel in your body?").

- Reinforce that identity is not static—it evolves with nervous system healing.

4. Grief Co-Regulation Protocol (Partner or Practitioner-Facilitated)
Purpose: Regulate dysregulation through safe connection
Instructions:
- Sit across from the client with soft eye contact (if tolerated).

- Mirror slow breathing and gently rock or sway together.

- Add optional vocalizations (e.g., low humming) to activate the vagus nerve.

- After 2–3 minutes, invite the client to name any shift in sensation, emotion, or presence.

5. Nature Prescription
Purpose: Encourage nervous system regulation through natural environments
Instructions:
- Assign weekly nature-based grief rituals (e.g., sitting near a tree, walking barefoot, placing a memory stone in a body of water).

- Guide clients to notice body shifts during and after the experience.

- Journal reflections or body responses to deepen interoception and symbolic integration.

References
Bonanno, G. A. (2009). *The other side of sadness: What the new science of bereavement tells us about life after loss.* Basic Books.

Coan, J. A., Schaefer, H. S., & Davidson, R. J. (2006). Lending a hand: Social regulation of the neural response to threat. *Psychological Science, 17*(12), 1032–1039. https://doi.org/10.1111/j.1467-9280.2006.01832.x

Damasio, A. (1999). *The feeling of what happens: Body and emotion in the making of consciousness.* Harcourt.

Gendlin, E. T. (1982). *Focusing.* Bantam.

Levine, P. A. (2010). *In an unspoken voice: How the body releases trauma and restores goodness.* North Atlantic Books.

Neimeyer, R. A. (2000). Searching for the meaning of meaning:

Grief therapy and the process of reconstruction. *Death Studies, 24*(6), 541–558. https://doi.org/10.1080/07481180050121480

Porges, S. W. (2011). *The polyvagal theory: Neurophysiological foundations of emotions, attachment, communication, and self-regulation.* W. W. Norton & Company.

Schore, A. N. (2003). *Affect dysregulation and disorders of the self.* W. W. Norton & Company.

Stolorow, R. D. (2007). *Trauma and human existence: Autobiographical, psychoanalytic, and philosophical reflections.* Routledge.

Van der Kolk, B. A. (2014). *The body keeps the score: Brain, mind, and body in the healing of trauma.* Viking.

CHAPTER 15

Habit Change & Addictive Behavior

Predictive Processing and Habit Loops

Habits are not moral failings or willpower deficiencies. They are neural efficiencies built through **predictive processing**: the brain's attempt to minimize uncertainty by automating familiar patterns. The nervous system favors what is predictable, not necessarily what is beneficial.

From a Neurosomatic Intelligence (NSI) lens, habits —whether supportive or destructive—are encoded through **repetition and state association**. This means behaviors are often reinforced not just by outcome (reward), but by the internal state they emerge from: stress, boredom, fatigue, shame.

When the nervous system anticipates dysregulation, it searches for the quickest path to relief. This prediction isn't conscious—it is a learned efficiency developed over time. The body begins to associate specific sensations (like tension or fatigue) with specific behaviors (like scrolling or snacking) as a way to restore balance—even if only temporarily.

The brain's **predictive model** uses past experience to anticipate future internal states and activate pre-learned behavioral loops. These loops become stronger with repetition and are stored deep within implicit memory systems, making them resistant to cognitive override alone.

The Habit Loop:

1. **Cue:** A physiological or emotional signal (e.g., tension, loneliness)
2. **Routine:** The behavior (e.g., scrolling, bingeing, drinking)
3. **Reward:** Temporary relief or shift in nervous system state

This loop becomes hardwired over time, especially when paired with **sympathetic activation** (urgency, stress) or **dorsal collapse** (numbing, shutdown). The reward isn't always pleasure—it's often a decrease in discomfort.

NSI focuses not on erasing habits through cognitive force, but on **interrupting the loop somatically**—starting with the cue. We teach the body to feel the signal, pause in safety, and choose differently. This creates a pathway for change rooted in regulation, not resistance.

Case Study: Digital Scrolling and Dissociative Loops – The Story of Aimee

"Aimee", a 27-year-old creative entrepreneur, came to NSI work to address chronic screen time and emotional disconnection.

She described "scrolling until she felt numb," often for hours before bed. What she labeled as procrastination or laziness was actually a **freeze-based pattern**. Her body associated stillness with risk, so she filled silence with stimulation.

Intervention:
- Tracked **cue states**—numbing and emptiness before the scroll began.

- Introduced **pre-pattern rituals** of tactile stimulation (stone rolling, textured blankets) and **self-touch anchoring** during nighttime.

- Practiced **visual orienting** to expand awareness and reduce tunnel vision before reaching for her phone.

Clinician Note:

Aimee's scrolling was not distraction—it was **dissociation management**. By giving her nervous system other ways to feel "held" in stillness, she began to reclaim nighttime as a space for integration rather than avoidance.

Nervous System Rewiring vs. Cognitive Force

Traditional behavior change models often rely heavily on **cognitive strategies** such as willpower, goal setting, and reframing. While these tools have merit, they are limited in their effectiveness when applied to nervous systems shaped by trauma, chronic stress, or dysregulation. For these individuals, top-down control can feel like **internalized coercion**—an attempt to force compliance from a body that is still protecting itself.

From a Neurosomatic Intelligence (NSI) perspective, attempting to override a deeply embedded habit without first addressing the body's state can trigger **backlash, emotional flooding, or shutdown**. These aren't signs of failure—they are signs of nervous system overload. When the internal system does not feel safe, new strategies are interpreted as threat, not growth.

Instead of pushing change through mental override, NSI invites a **bottom-up approach** that respects the body's need for safety, sequencing, and slowness. Key principles include:

- **State Before Strategy:** Regulation is the prerequisite for transformation. Before initiating change, the nervous system must shift out of survival mode. Otherwise, any new behavior—no matter how positive—can feel dangerous to the subconscious system. Safety first, always.

- **Somatic Substitution:** Behaviors are rarely random; they serve a **neurobiological need**, such as soothing, stimulation, or connection. Rather than removing the habit, we offer an alternative somatic pathway to fulfill that need. For example, someone who uses food to regulate overwhelm might substitute with rocking, grounding, or vocalization to downshift their nervous system state.

- **Titration:** The nervous system does not respond well to abrupt shifts. Instead of radical overhauls, NSI practices emphasize **gradual exposure to change**, allowing the system to build tolerance, resilience, and trust. Micro-shifts, done consistently, produce sustainable rewiring.

In this way, NSI treats habit change not as an act of mental discipline but as an act of **nervous system compassion**. The goal is not to "fix" the behavior, but to **free** the system from the state that keeps defaulting to it. When the body feels **safe**, change becomes possible. When the body feels **heard**, change becomes lasting.

Case Study: Smoking and State Regulation – The Journey of Dashon

"Dashon", a 46-year-old Black man with complex childhood trauma, had been smoking cigarettes since age 14.

He had tried quitting several times but always relapsed during stress. NSI revealed that **smoking was his most consistent regulation tool**—a rare moment of full breath, pause, and oral soothing. Quitting without replacing that somatic need only activated threat.

Intervention:

- Shifted the focus from "quitting" to **nervous system regulation**.

- Taught **urge surfing** with a somatic anchor—holding a cinnamon stick between his lips while practicing 4-count box breathing.

- Built a **replacement ritual** of vocal toning with music, creating vibrational exhale stimulation similar to the breath-hold/release of smoking.

Clinician Note:
Dashon's nervous system needed familiarity. By recreating the breath rhythm and sensory input of smoking without the substance, we honored his nervous system's need for pacing and containment. Quitting became possible not through force, but through **neurobiological replacement**.

Sustainable Change Through Body-Based Cues

Sustainable behavior change begins with **body awareness**, not thought correction. By tracking internal signals (interoception), we can learn to intervene earlier in the habit loop—before automatic behaviors kick in.

NSI Practices Include:

- **Urge Surfing:** Notice the physical sensation of an urge without acting on it; track its rise, peak, and decline. This increases distress tolerance and shows the nervous system that urges are temporary and survivable.

- **Pre-Pattern Pausing:** Inhabit a micro-moment of stillness when the cue arises. This pause disrupts the autopilot loop, giving the body a chance to choose something different. Even a few seconds of conscious awareness can create space for new wiring.

- **Replacement Rituals:** Engage in an alternative somatic act (e.g., humming, shaking, walking, self-touch) that satisfies the nervous system. These rituals are not distractions—they are re-patterning tools that help rewire association by fulfilling the underlying need in a regulated way.

- **Safety Mapping:** Identify when, where, and with whom the system feels safe enough to make changes. This creates a nervous system-informed strategy that honors state-dependent learning and prioritizes choice over pressure.

These practices work by building **bottom-up capacity**—the foundation for top-down decision-making. Over time, the nervous system learns: "I can pause. I can choose. I am not at the mercy of my patterns." With enough safety and repetition, the body begins to anticipate regulation—not reactivity—as its default mode.

Case Study: Rewiring Emotional Eating – The Story of Tasha

"Tasha", a 39-year-old trauma survivor, had struggled with late-night binge eating for over a decade.
Her pattern always began with loneliness or overstimulation at the end of the day. Evenings brought a flood of unprocessed emotion, which she quieted with food. Despite multiple diets and cognitive interventions, the binge cycle continued.

Through NSI, we identified that her binge episodes were rooted in a **dorsal vagal shutdown** state. Her nervous system had learned that stillness = threat, and food provided stimulation and grounding. Cognitive approaches had failed because they bypassed the physiological pattern.

Intervention:
- Introduced **pre-pattern pausing**—placing her hand on

her chest, humming, and naming sensations when the urge began.

- Practiced **somatic substitution**: replacing eating with rhythmic rocking, hand compression, and warm tea (offering sensory input and safety).

- Co-created **safety mapping** to identify evenings when she could connect with a trusted friend or pet before the urge arose.

Clinician Note:
Tasha didn't need more control—she needed **interoceptive reconnection**. Her binge behavior was not self-sabotage, but a coping strategy for nervous system overwhelm. Once her body learned that she could safely pause, her urges decreased by 60% within six weeks.

Repatterning for Freedom

True habit change is not a war waged against the self—it is a reunion with the body. Neurosomatic Intelligence teaches us that patterns are not the problem; they are the body's best attempt at safety and regulation with the tools it had at the time. When we shift our approach from cognitive control to somatic curiosity, we stop asking, "How do I fix this?" and start asking, "What does my body need in this moment?"

The path to lasting change is not paved with force, but with felt safety. By learning to track our cues, regulate our states, and offer our nervous system new options, we create not just behavioral shifts—but embodied freedom. Change becomes not a punishment or performance, but a form of self-trust.

This is how we move from survival-based compulsions into self-led choice. Not by silencing the body, but by listening to it.

Trauma-Informed NSI Practitioner Toolkit

To support clients in sustainable habit change and recovery from addictive patterns, NSI practitioners can integrate the following trauma-informed tools:

1. State-Tracking Journal
Encourage clients to document sensations, emotional states, and behaviors to build interoceptive awareness and notice patterns.

2. Regulation First Protocol
Begin sessions with grounding exercises—such as orienting, breathwork, or bilateral stimulation—to downshift the nervous system before exploring change.

3. Somatic Anchors Cheat Sheet
Provide a personalized list of somatic anchors (e.g., favorite textures, movements, or breath rhythms) that help the client return to regulation.

4. Pattern Interruption Plans
Collaboratively create micro-practices clients can use in the moment of craving or compulsion (e.g., drink water, place hand on heart, hum 3 tones).

5. Body-Based Goal Mapping
Support clients in setting nervous system-aligned goals by identifying which behaviors create true safety, satisfaction, and connection.

6. Shame Recovery Integration
Normalize setbacks. Use compassionate inquiry and somatic resourcing to transform shame into curiosity and choice.

7. Co-Regulation Strategy
Identify safe people, pets, or community resources that help the client's nervous system stabilize when dysregulated.

These tools center the body as an ally—not an obstacle—in the change process. When clients feel their way into new patterns, transformation becomes both safe and sustainable.

References

Bessel van der Kolk. (2014). *The body keeps the score: Brain, mind, and body in the healing of trauma.* Viking.

Craig, A. D. (2002). How do you feel? Interoception: the sense of the physiological condition of the body. *Nature Reviews Neuroscience, 3*(8), 655–666. https://doi.org/10.1038/nrn894

Damasio, A. (1999). *The feeling of what happens: Body and emotion in the making of consciousness.* Harcourt.

Friston, K. (2010). The free-energy principle: A unified brain theory? *Nature Reviews Neuroscience, 11*(2), 127–138. https://doi.org/10.1038/nrn2787

Levine, P. A. (2010). *In an unspoken voice: How the body releases trauma and restores goodness.* North Atlantic Books.

Porges, S. W. (2011). *The polyvagal theory: Neurophysiological foundations of emotions, attachment, communication, and self-regulation.* W. W. Norton & Company.

Sapolsky, R. M. (2004). *Why zebras don't get ulcers: The acclaimed guide to stress, stress-related diseases, and coping* (3rd ed.). Henry Holt and Company.

Siegel, D. J. (2012). *The developing mind: How relationships and the brain interact to shape who we are* (2nd ed.). The Guilford Press.

Van der Kolk, B. A., & Najavits, L. M. (2013). Clinical implications of neuroscience research in PTSD. *Psychiatric Annals, 43*(6), 292–295. https://doi.org/10.3928/00485713-20130605-06

CHAPTER 16

Visibility, Presence, and Connection

The Fear of Being Seen: Relational Trauma and Visibility

Being seen—*truly* seen—is both a human longing and a primal threat for many individuals with relational trauma. Visibility holds the promise of connection, affirmation, and belonging—but it also holds the memory of exposure, humiliation, or betrayal.

For those raised in environments where vulnerability was met with criticism or abandonment, the nervous system learns that expression equals risk. The act of being noticed becomes paired with fear, and over time, the body encodes this threat into its default survival strategy.

Visibility as a Threat Response

Relational trauma doesn't just influence how we think about ourselves—it wires our nervous system to anticipate danger in social engagement. This often manifests as:

- **Chronic self-monitoring:** Constantly scanning for how one is perceived or judged

- **Social withdrawal or masking:** Avoiding presence to remain safe

- **People-pleasing and over-accommodation:** Suppressing needs to maintain harmony

- **Fear of being "too much" or "not enough":** Ingrained

shame-based narratives that shrink authentic expression

These are not personality traits—they are *protective adaptations*. The nervous system, attempting to avoid further pain, limits one's presence in the room, in the relationship, and in their own body.

The NSI Perspective

From a Neurosomatic Intelligence (NSI) lens, visibility is not a cognitive mindset shift—it is a **somatic recalibration**. We cannot simply affirm our way into presence; we must *feel* our way into it.

When the body has experienced social connection as dangerous, it requires titrated exposure to being seen. This includes:

- Rebuilding tolerance for eye contact

- Practicing vocal tone and volume

- Engaging in gentle movements that foster openness (e.g., expansive posture, relaxed facial expression)

NSI teaches that presence with others must begin with safety within. The body must first become a safe home before it can be shared with the world.

Healing visibility wounds means learning that:

- Your presence is not a threat

- Your voice is not a liability

- Your needs are not a burden

This is not just emotional healing—it is neural repatterning. It is the body rewriting the story that *being seen is dangerous*, and replacing it with: *I can be seen and still be safe.*

Somatic Safety in Expression

Authentic expression is one of the most courageous acts of embodiment. Whether it's stating a need, setting a boundary, crying in front of another, or even laughing freely, these moments require the nervous system to feel safe enough to be vulnerable. Yet for many individuals with a history of trauma, particularly relational or developmental trauma, expression has been historically linked with danger or rejection.

When the nervous system is in a state of defense—fight, flight, freeze, or fawn—authentic expression is often muted, monitored, or entirely suppressed. The voice may tremble or disappear, the body may brace or shrink, and the individual may default to appeasing or performative behavior in order to avoid perceived threat.

The Neurosomatic Reframe

Neurosomatic Intelligence (NSI) reframes expression not as a purely psychological or communication issue, but as a *state-dependent somatic skill*. Simply put, we cannot express authentically when the body does not feel safe. Therefore, the path to reclaiming our voice begins with **regulation**, not rehearsal.

Expression is a function of neurophysiological safety. NSI helps clients build capacity for:

- **Vocalization without collapse**: Exploring tone, pitch, and volume in a way that engages the vagus nerve without overwhelming the system.

- **Eye contact with attunement**: Practicing mutual gaze that feels connected, not invasive—especially important for those with a history of being shamed or ignored.

- **Spontaneity without fear**: Restoring the ability to improvise, joke, dance, or speak freely without anticipating ridicule or punishment.

These capacities do not develop through force, but through titration, safety, and practice.

Core Somatic Practices

To rebuild expressive safety, NSI includes the following bottom-up interventions:

- **Vagal Toning:** Humming, chanting, singing, or even buzzing sounds help stimulate the vagus nerve and calm the limbic system. These vibrations regulate breathing, heart rate, and vocal confidence.

- **Facial Play:** Gentle micro-movements of the face —wiggling the eyebrows, softening the jaw, massaging the temples—help unwind chronic facial bracing often associated with suppression or self-monitoring.

- **Mirror Presence Practice:** Looking into a mirror and meeting your own gaze with softness, curiosity, or affirming words begins to rewire internalized shame. This practice can help repattern the fear of judgment and cultivate self-acceptance.

- **Safe Vocal Play:** Making nonsensical sounds, singing in the shower, or reading aloud in expressive tones helps restore spontaneity and reduce vocal inhibition.

Repatterning Expression

Over time, these practices shift the body's association with expression from *threat* to *possibility*. Neural and muscular patterns begin to rewire in ways that support congruent, confident presence. The voice becomes less about performance and more about embodiment. Words carry weight, not fear. Emotions become shareable, not suppressible.

Expression is not about being loud or charismatic—it's about being **present and congruent**. When our voice aligns with our truth, and our body feels safe enough to let that truth emerge, we experience expression as liberation, not liability.

Building Secure Social and Spiritual Attachments

Connection is not merely an emotional experience—it is a neurobiological necessity. From the earliest stages of life, our nervous systems are shaped by the presence (or absence) of attuned, consistent caregivers. When those early relationships provided safety, responsiveness, and mirroring, we developed secure attachment patterns that support healthy intimacy, expression, and self-trust. But when care was inconsistent, neglectful, or harmful, the nervous system adapted—often by associating closeness with danger, unpredictability, or pain.

Trauma and Attachment Disruption

For many trauma survivors, adult relationships can trigger the same survival responses once used to navigate childhood environments:

- **Avoidance** to protect against rejection or engulfment

- **Anxious over-functioning** to maintain closeness at the expense of self

- **Fawning** to appease and preserve connection

- **Dissociation or emotional numbing** to avoid vulnerability

These behaviors are not failures of character—they are

brilliant survival strategies. However, they can limit one's capacity to receive support, build trust, or feel truly seen in community.

From a **Neurosomatic Intelligence (NSI)** perspective, secure attachment is not just a psychological concept—it's a **state of regulation**. We feel safe with others when our nervous system has the capacity to co-regulate, repair rupture, and remain anchored in the face of emotional intensity.

Rebuilding Attachment: A Somatic Pathway

Attachment repair requires both **external connection** and **internal reparenting**. It is the dual process of being safely witnessed and learning to meet ourselves with presence.

Co-Regulation (Social Repair):

- Practicing safety in relationships where presence, breath, voice, and rhythm are consistent and non-threatening

- Sharing space with emotionally regulated others who model containment, empathy, and stability

- Allowing nervous system synchrony through shared experiences like walking, music, eye contact, or safe touch

Reparenting (Internal Repair):

- Learning to speak to yourself with compassion, structure, and affirmation

- Creating boundaries and rituals that offer a sense of containment and predictability

- Meeting unmet needs with present-moment care: soothing, validating, and protecting the parts of you that never received this in childhood

Attachment rewiring does not happen in isolation—it happens in small, safe, repeated interactions that signal to the body: *This is different. This is safe. You are not alone anymore.*

The Role of Spiritual Attachment

For those who have experienced significant relational rupture, connection to something larger—**spirit, nature, ancestors, community, or divinity**—can offer a powerful anchor of safety and meaning. This is not bypassing human intimacy; it is expanding the nervous system's relational landscape.

Spiritual attachment can look like:

- Feeling held by the earth while resting in nature

- Connecting with ancestral wisdom or guidance

- Experiencing prayer, ritual, or meditation as a co-regulatory act

- Engaging with a spiritual community that honors your story and worth

These connections offer **non-transactional presence**—you are not required to perform, fix, or achieve in order to belong.

Reclaiming Belonging

When both social and spiritual nervous system anchors are strengthened, the body receives new messages:

- *"I am not too much."*

- *"I do not have to earn love."*

- *"I can ask for help and stay in connection."*

- *"I can trust myself and others."*

This embodied sense of safety and belonging becomes the foundation for expression, intimacy, and presence. Healing attachment wounds is not about becoming more agreeable or independent—it is about becoming more **authentically you** in relationship to others and the sacred.

The Integration of Presence

Presence is not perfection. It is not the absence of discomfort, triggers, or dysregulation. Rather, presence is the *return*—the embodied decision to come back to the here-and-now with curiosity, compassion, and choice. It is a practice, not a personality trait. And it is cultivated through the nervous system, not forced through willpower.

For individuals healing from relational trauma, presence can feel dangerous. The body may associate presence with exposure or vulnerability. But as we build somatic safety through Neurosomatic Intelligence (NSI) practices, presence becomes more accessible. It no longer requires performance or hypervigilance—it becomes a natural byproduct of regulation.

Presence as a Practice of Reclamation

Presence allows us to:

- Speak truth without abandoning the body

- Witness others without collapsing into their emotions

- Set boundaries with clarity and kindness

- Show up in our fullness—not as a mask, but as a mirror of authenticity

In NSI work, presence is reclaimed not through mental discipline, but through **repetition, repair, and relational safety**. We do not aim to be present all the time—we aim to return faster, with less shame, and with greater integration each time we leave.

Visibility as Liberation

When clients and practitioners reclaim the right to be seen, they do more than heal their individual nervous systems—they disrupt generational and cultural patterns of invisibility, suppression, and self-erasure. They interrupt the legacy of silence that told them to stay small, stay quiet, stay compliant.

Every time someone:

- Uses their voice after years of silence

- Shows up authentically in a space where they once masked

- Chooses connection over withdrawal

- Receives love without shrinking

—they declare that presence is possible, even after trauma.

This is the liberation NSI offers: not a perfect nervous system, but a present one. Not a life without pain, but a life with more capacity to feel, hold, and metabolize what is true.

Practitioner's Reflection: Reclaiming Visibility as Sacred Nervous System Work

As a trauma-informed practitioner, I've witnessed countless moments where the most powerful breakthroughs did not come from cognitive insight—but from a trembling voice finally spoken aloud, a gaze held for the first time without fear, or a breath taken without collapse. These moments may seem small, but they are nothing short of revolutionary.

Visibility work is not about performance. It is about presence. It's about rebuilding the inner scaffolding that allows a person to *be with themselves*—and *then* with the world—without bracing, masking, or hiding.

In my own healing and in the work with clients, I have learned that the fear of being seen is often the residue of unacknowledged brilliance. What was once punished as "too much" or "not enough" was often a sacred expression of truth, creativity, or emotional wisdom.

As practitioners, we are not just helping others express more—we are helping their bodies *believe* that expression is safe. We model presence by embodying it ourselves. We co-regulate safety, not with perfect words, but with attuned breath, regulated tone, and unwavering permission for clients to exist fully.

The nervous system does not speak in language—it speaks in *felt experience*. And when we honor that, healing becomes not just possible—but inevitable.

Let presence be the medicine.
Let visibility be the revolution.

References

Maté, G. (2008). *In the realm of hungry ghosts: Close encounters with addiction.* North Atlantic Books.

Neff, K. (2011). *Self-compassion: The proven power of being kind to yourself.* William Morrow.

Porges, S. W. (2011). *The polyvagal theory: Neurophysiological foundations of emotions, attachment, communication, and self-regulation.* W. W. Norton & Company.

Van der Kolk, B. (2014). *The body keeps the score: Brain, mind, and* *body in the healing of trauma.* Viking.

Siegel, D. J. (2012). *The developing mind: How relationships and the brain interact to shape who we are* (2nd ed.). The Guilford Press.

CONCLUSION

The Body Remembers… and Rewires

*Reclaiming the Nervous System. Rewriting the Story.
Returning to Self. Rewired for Resilience.*

The Adaptive Intelligence of the Nervous System

The human nervous system is not inherently flawed or broken. Rather, it is a dynamic, adaptive system designed to ensure survival in the presence of perceived threat. When individuals experience chronic stress, trauma, or relational disruptions—particularly during developmentally sensitive periods—the nervous system makes intelligent adjustments to maximize safety, minimize harm, and preserve internal equilibrium. These responses are not malfunctions; they are evidence of the body's brilliance under duress.

Responses such as dissociation, emotional shutdown, hypervigilance, compulsive behaviors, or appeasement patterns (commonly identified as the "fawn response") emerge as strategic adaptations. They reflect the nervous system's effort to protect the individual when fight or flight were not viable or safe. These autonomic patterns are not evidence of dysfunction, but of coherence—internal logic born from the body's imperative to survive.

Understanding trauma responses through the lens of neuroscience and polyvagal theory (Porges, 2011) reframes them from being symptomatic of pathology to being indicators of resilience and neuroplasticity. The system is doing exactly what it was designed to do: protect the organism. However, these once-adaptive responses may persist long after the original threat has passed, creating a mismatch between current reality and somatic reactivity.

It is critical to recognize that **survival is not the final chapter** in the narrative of healing. The arc of transformation extends beyond endurance. While survival strategies allow individuals to continue functioning under threat, true healing invites a reorganization of the nervous system—one that allows for regulation, flexibility, and deeper relational engagement.

This next phase—**the shift from survival to integration**—requires a body-based approach that fosters safety, capacity building, and sensory awareness. Neurosomatic Intelligence (NSI) offers this framework, guiding individuals to move from automatic reactivity to empowered presence. In doing so, the nervous system is not only stabilized but reconditioned to support aliveness, connection, and choice.

Ultimately, the goal is not to discard or deny survival patterns, but to honor their origins and gently unwind them with compassion. Only then can we access the full spectrum of human experience—rest, joy, intimacy, creativity, and meaning—and restore coherence not only within the nervous system, but across the narrative of the self.

Reclaiming Your Nervous System: A Return to Embodied Relationship

This book has outlined the foundational principles of **Neurosomatic Intelligence (NSI)**, presenting an integrated framework that situates trauma, attachment wounding, chronic stress, and sociocultural adversity within the neurobiological architecture of the human experience. Rather than pathologizing emotional dysregulation, dissociative tendencies, or behavioral compulsions, NSI reframes them as evidence of the nervous system's **adaptive intelligence**—patterns developed to ensure survival in environments where safety was absent or inconsistent.

Throughout this text, we have explored how the nervous system encodes experience not only cognitively but somatically. Dissociation, anxiety, hypervigilance, reactivity, people-pleasing, shame-based inhibition, and self-sabotaging loops are not simply maladaptive habits—they are **neurophysiological responses** to unprocessed threat. These embodied patterns reflect the body's attempt to maintain coherence under pressure, often solidifying during early developmental windows when relational safety, attuned co-regulation, and secure attachment may have been disrupted (Schore, 2012; Van der Kolk, 2014).

To **reclaim the nervous system** is not to override, silence, or eradicate these patterns. Rather, it is a call to **re-enter relationship** with the body—not as a mechanical system to be controlled, but as a living organism capable of restoration, integration, and growth. It is a shift from top-down dominance to bottom-up collaboration. This reclamation process involves:

- **Somatic attunement**: learning to listen to interoceptive and exteroceptive signals with curiosity rather than criticism

- **Pattern completion**: supporting the resolution of previously interrupted stress responses through movement, breath, and relational safety

- **State scaffolding**: building new regulatory pathways through practices that anchor the system in safety, not suppression

By establishing consistent **signals of safety**—through breathwork, co-regulation, movement, stillness, and sensory anchoring—the nervous system gradually reorganizes its internal maps. This transformation does not require force or perfection, but **presence**. Healing becomes less about "doing more" and more about **being with**—with sensation, with history, with discomfort, and ultimately with self.

Through the lens of NSI, **healing is not linear**. It is recursive, dynamic, and deeply relational. The nervous system may oscillate between states of expansion and contraction, regulation and dysregulation. But with practice, safety becomes more accessible. Response flexibility improves. And the body—once seen as unpredictable or even threatening—becomes a trusted ally.

This is the essence of **nervous system reclamation:**

- A movement away from adversarial self-control

- A shift toward embodied sovereignty

- A return to relational wholeness

The body does not need to be fixed—it needs to be **felt**, honored, and co-regulated. Reclaiming your nervous system is, ultimately, an act of **remembering**—of who you were before adaptation took precedence, and who you are becoming as regulation and resonance return.

Becoming the Embodied Version of Yourself: From Adaptation to Self-Authorship

Embodiment is not a static destination; rather, it is a **recursive and relational process** of coming into full contact with one's internal state—physiologically, emotionally, and sensorially. It reflects the capacity to attune to one's nervous system with discernment, to respond with intention rather than impulse, and to live in congruence with one's inner experience, not in reaction to it.

Within the **Neurosomatic Intelligence (NSI)** framework, embodiment begins with **interoceptive restoration**—the process of reclaiming access to the body's subtle signals such as breath, muscle tone, heart rate variability, and visceral sensations. These signals, often blunted or distorted in the context of trauma or chronic stress (Craig, 2002; Khalsa et al., 2018), are essential for navigating moment-to-moment states and making informed choices about boundaries, needs, and relationships.

Importantly, NSI emphasizes a **bottom-up orientation to transformation**. Rather than relying exclusively on cognitive reappraisal or behavioral willpower, practitioners and clients cultivate change through the somatic pathways of safety, rhythm, and regulation. This orientation fosters neuroplasticity from within, allowing previously dysregulated systems to develop **greater flexibility, resilience, and integration** over time (Porges, 2011; Siegel, 2020).

Key markers of embodied transformation include:

- **Self-regulatory capacity**: The ability to shift states without dissociation, collapse, or compulsion

- **Threshold honoring**: Recognizing and respecting one's limits without guilt or override

- **Somatic agency**: Making choices informed by body awareness, not trauma imprint

- **Expressive congruence**: Aligning emotional expression with authentic inner state

To **become the embodied version of oneself** is to move beyond the identity shaped by chronic survival responses. It is to transition from self-protection to self-possession—from being reflexively driven by the past to **intentionally present** in the now. This transformation is not about erasing the effects of trauma but **re-contextualizing them** as part of one's nervous system story, while cultivating a future governed not by fear but by felt safety.

Over time, the embodied self that emerges is characterized not by hyper-vigilance or shutdown, but by **capacity, connection, and coherence**. In this state, individuals no longer treat their body as an adversary or liability. Instead, the body becomes a partner in discernment, a barometer of alignment, and a site of liberation.

Embodiment, then, is an act of **self-authorship**—a reclamation of one's internal narrative and neurobiological rhythm. It is the capacity to say:

"I feel. I choose. I belong to myself."

And in that declaration, a new version of self is born—not one defined by trauma, but by **agency, authenticity, and relational wholeness**.

The Invitation to Wholeness: A Somatic Integration of Healing and Agency

As this journey culminates, the reader is not ushered toward a definitive conclusion but rather welcomed into a **living continuum of somatic self-inquiry and regulation**. Healing, through the lens of Neurosomatic Intelligence (NSI), is not a fixed endpoint but a dynamic process—a rhythm, a conversation, and an invitation that unfolds in the present moment, over and over again.

This invitation is not rooted in clinical abstraction, but in **embodied praxis**. It calls the individual to engage with the nervous system not as a set of problems to be solved, but as a *living intelligence* to be honored, attuned to, and co-authored with. The invitation is to:

- **Reclaim the rhythm of breath** as a regulatory anchor, restoring vagal tone and coherence in moments of overwhelm (Porges, 2011).

- **Cultivate internal safety** amidst external instability, by increasing one's capacity to pendulate between activation and restoration.

- **Honor grief and joy** as biologically valid and somatically housed experiences—both essential to emotional metabolism and narrative integration (Levine, 2010; Van der Kolk, 2014).

- **Return to felt sense over force**, and to relational attunement over cognitive control, building neurobiological trust through presence and interoceptive precision.

Healing through NSI is not about erasing or overriding the past. Rather, it is about **compassionate integration**—weaving the threads of trauma, adaptation, and resilience into a more coherent whole. It is a form of post-traumatic growth that does not bypass pain, but metabolizes it into wisdom, capacity, and relational depth.

The nervous system, once organized around survival imperatives, can be **reshaped through intentional relational and somatic inputs**. The plasticity of the human system means that even entrenched patterns can shift—not through willpower, but through safety, repetition, and supported practice (Sapolsky, 2017; Siegel, 2020).

This is the **revolution of Neurosomatic Intelligence**:

Not healing through disconnection, but through relationship.

Not through suppression, but through expression.
Not through perfection, but through presence.

This is the **remembering of the body's brilliance**—a brilliance that was never lost, only obscured by adaptations too intelligent to be pathologized.

This is the **reclamation of selfhood**—a self once fragmented by relational and systemic ruptures, now slowly and somatically reassembled.

You are not what happened to you.
You are what is possible through you.
You are whole.
You are worthy.
You are wired for safety.

And you are ready to rise—not by becoming someone new, but by returning to who you've always been beneath the survival strategies.

PRACTITIONER'S AFTERWORD
The Sacred Work of Witnessing, Rewiring, and Reclaiming

By Dr. Deilen Michelle Villegas, Ph.D.
Board-Certified Holistic Health & Wellness Practitioner |Traumatic Stress Expert| Clinical Mental Health Counselor | Certified Clinical Sexologist | Neurosomatic Educator

As this text comes to a close, it is essential to acknowledge the significance of the reader's journey—not merely through the intellectual exploration of Neurosomatic Intelligence (NSI), but through the embodied engagement required to metabolize trauma and reclaim nervous system agency. To have reached this point implies more than cognitive interest; it reflects a willingness to sit with discomfort, to listen to the body's signals, and to choose regulation over reactivity. This is not a passive reading experience. It is an act of embodied participation and personal reclamation.

From a clinical perspective, trauma disrupts the body's capacity for integration. It fragments memory, dulls interoception, and often erodes the internal sense of safety required for healing. Yet healing does not demand perfection or linear progress. It requires presence. It necessitates creating conditions—physiological and relational—that allow the nervous system to downshift from chronic survival into self-attunement and co-regulation.

As a practitioner, I approach this work not only through academic training and clinical application, but through lived experience. Personal history informs professional integrity. Like many of my clients and colleagues, I have witnessed the impact of hypervigilance, shame-based self-monitoring, and somatic collapse. I have also experienced the transformational power of restoring parasympathetic access, of co-creating safety in therapeutic containers, and of engaging in practices that bring the body back online—back into relationship with itself and with others.

Healing, therefore, is not about "fixing" what is broken. Rather, it is a cyclical, somatic process of remembering. The body does not forget its history—but with attuned support, it can rewire its response. NSI-based protocols recognize this capacity and offer a roadmap to cultivate embodiment through titrated exposure, sensory anchoring, and relational repair. Over time, these practices re-pattern not only the nervous system's internal landscape but also the relational templates we carry forward.

In therapeutic settings, we see clients return to their sense of agency not through cognitive reframing alone, but through subtle physiological shifts: a longer exhale, a softened jaw, a grounded gaze. These are not minor victories. They are neurological milestones marking the reclamation of safety, worth, and wholeness.

To the reader—whether clinician, client, or seeker—your journey through this material is a declaration of sovereignty. It affirms that healing is not reserved for those with ideal circumstances, but for those who commit to honoring their nervous system's wisdom.

As we integrate the insights of NSI into broader healing modalities, we remember this truth:

> *The body remembers—and it also rewires.*
> *It carries the imprint of what was, and the possibility of what can be.*

This duality is what makes the work of trauma recovery so

sacred. It is not solely about restoration—it is about evolution. May this work continue to support those who are ready not just to survive, but to live, love, and lead from an embodied place of power and peace.

The Role of the Practitioner: From Fixer to Facilitator

In trauma-informed, body-based approaches to healing, the role of the practitioner shifts fundamentally from that of an expert who diagnoses and corrects, to a facilitator who co-regulates, witnesses, and supports somatic restoration. Within the framework of Neurosomatic Intelligence (NSI), the practitioner's task is not to impose change, but to create conditions in which the client's nervous system can safely expand its capacity for regulation, embodiment, and relational presence.

Rather than focusing on pathology or deficit, this model emphasizes physiological literacy and adaptive intelligence. Practitioners are trained to recognize survival responses—such as dissociation, hypervigilance, or emotional reactivity—not as signs of dysfunction, but as the body's intelligent strategies for managing overwhelming threat. In this context, behavior is interpreted not solely through cognitive frameworks, but through nervous system states.

Somatic attunement becomes a cornerstone of the practitioner's skillset. This involves sensing and responding to subtle shifts in breath, posture, facial expression, and tone— not to interpret or correct, but to co-regulate. The therapeutic relationship becomes a vehicle for neurophysiological safety, where healing occurs not through directive strategies, but through embodied presence, rhythmic synchronization, and titrated return to self.

NSI emphasizes that healing occurs in *state*, not merely in strategy. This principle guides practitioners to meet clients where they are physiologically, rather than where they are expected to be cognitively. Interventions are tailored to the client's current window of tolerance, ensuring that practices are not retraumatizing, but capacity-building.

Ultimately, the practitioner's role is to hold a regulated container for exploration, to mirror safety and worth, and to support the body in remembering what it feels like to be whole. This shift—from fixer to facilitator—redefines the therapeutic alliance and honors the wisdom inherent in every nervous system.

What It Means to Hold Space

In the context of trauma-informed, somatic healing, *holding space* refers to the intentional practice of offering attuned, non-intrusive presence to individuals as they engage in vulnerable emotional processing. This act extends beyond passive support; it represents a neurobiological commitment to co-regulation, boundary honoring, and the suspension of premature intervention.

Holding space involves several core capacities:

- **Emotional Witnessing Without Intervention:** Allowing expressions of grief, fear, or anger to unfold without attempting to soothe, correct, or redirect the experience.

- **Nonjudgmental Containment:** Providing a safe relational container in which dysregulated states—such as rage or sorrow—can be metabolized without eliciting shame or withdrawal.

- **Respect for Somatic Timing:** Recognizing that healing unfolds through physiological readiness, not cognitive timelines, and refraining from imposing externally driven expectations.

- **Boundary-Aware Support:** Avoiding the impulse to

rescue or override, particularly when a client is engaging in empowered self-reclamation or boundary-setting.

Within Neurosomatic Intelligence (NSI), holding space requires practitioners to embody both **regulatory resilience** and **relational neutrality**. The clinician's nervous system serves as an anchor, offering cues of safety through breath, posture, facial expression, and rhythm. This is not merely an emotional skill but a physiological offering; clients subconsciously borrow regulation from the provider's state of calm presence (Porges, 2011).

This work demands more than clinical competence. It requires a commitment to ongoing self-regulation and embodied awareness. Practitioners must be as **regulated as they are educated**, and as **present as they are prepared**. This alignment fosters trust and safety, allowing for the unfolding of deep relational repair.

When we hold space in this way, we become co-regulators, containers of integrity, and disruptors of generational shame. This is not simply therapeutic technique—it is a transformative act that reshapes relational blueprints and contributes to the healing of collective nervous system legacies.

From Trauma Stewardship to Transformation Stewardship: A Paradigm of Somatic Healing and Integrative Practice

Trauma-informed care requires more than theoretical knowledge of trauma's psychological and physiological impacts. It necessitates the capacity to remain somatically present with dysregulation and to support the gradual reintegration of a client's nervous system as it renegotiates safety, agency, and coherence (van der Kolk, 2014; Levine, 2010). Practitioners must be skilled not only in identifying trauma responses but in facilitating conditions under which the body can safely process and rewire those patterns.

However, a more expansive model is emerging within somatic and integrative healing disciplines—one that transcends trauma stewardship and moves toward what can be called *transformation stewardship*. This shift repositions the practitioner not solely as a guide through dysregulation and fragmentation, but as a facilitator of post-traumatic growth, embodied resilience, and reconnection with joy, purpose, and relational depth.

Transformation stewardship involves:

- Supporting the nervous system's movement beyond survival into expansion, creativity, and self-expression

- Holding space for the emergence of a new identity that is not defined by trauma but informed by integration

- Facilitating embodied experiences of pleasure, vitality, and belonging as valid endpoints of the healing journey

In this model, the practitioner acts as a somatic witness, a relational anchor, and a co-regulator—fostering both neurobiological repair and meaning reconstruction. While trauma stewardship focuses on mitigation of harm and stabilization, transformation stewardship emphasizes flourishing, wholeness, and the reclamation of life force.

This is not solely clinical work. It is interdisciplinary and deeply human: a convergence of physiological regulation, relational attunement, spiritual meaning-making, and legacy-building. It invites practitioners to hold both the suffering and the sacred in their work—recognizing that true healing often births not just recovery, but transformation.

The Practitioner as Instrument: Embodied Presence as a Therapeutic Modality

In the context of somatic and trauma-informed care, the practitioner is not an objective bystander but an integral component of the healing process. Emerging research in interpersonal neurobiology and co-regulation supports what seasoned clinicians have long observed: the practitioner's embodied presence directly influences the client's nervous system state (Siegel, 2012; Porges, 2011).

Every element of the practitioner—the tone of their voice, the cadence of their breath, the microexpressions of their face, and their capacity to remain regulated while in proximity to dysregulation—functions as a form of non-verbal intervention. These elements signal safety to the client's nervous system and create the conditions under which neuroplasticity and healing can occur.

This framework challenges traditional models that separate the practitioner from the process. Rather than relying exclusively on external techniques or cognitive strategies, it positions the *practitioner's state* as the primary tool of transformation. The body-to-body communication inherent in this dynamic plays a central role in creating therapeutic alliance, establishing co-regulation, and facilitating nervous system repair.

To serve in this role effectively, practitioners must engage in continual refinement of their own somatic awareness and regulatory capacity. This refinement is not pursued through perfectionism or emotional suppression but through intentional self-practice, personal integration work, and radical self-compassion.

Being the tool does not imply over-identification with the client's experience—it requires maintaining boundaries while offering attuned presence. In this way, the practitioner becomes a calibrated instrument of safety, resonance, and therapeutic change.

Practitioner Integration and Ethical Reverence

In trauma-informed, somatically-integrated practice, the practitioner's well-being is not peripheral—it is central to ethical and effective care. The nervous system of the clinician functions not only as a regulatory instrument for the client but as sacred technology in its own right, deserving of protection, attunement, and restoration.

Practitioners must be consistently reminded that this work does not demand martyrdom or self-sacrifice. Instead, it calls for rigorous boundary-setting, reciprocal care, and intentional embodiment of the principles offered to clients. Healing is not a unidirectional act; it is relational and bidirectional. The same principles that restore wholeness for those we serve must be honored within ourselves.

To remain in this field with integrity and longevity, we are required to return—again and again—to our own bodies, our breath, and our values. We must normalize practices that support our own regulation, co-regulation, and collective care. This is not ancillary—it is foundational.

May this serve as both a professional reminder and a personal affirmation:

That the practitioner deserves to be seen, supported, and healed. That nervous system health is a non-negotiable aspect of practitioner sustainability.

And that bearing witness to another's healing is a sacred act —one made possible by our own courageous commitment to embodiment, presence, and love.

With professional solidarity and deep reverence,
Dr. Deilen Michelle Villegas, Ph.D.
The Shamanic Goddess

Appendix A: Glossary Of Key Terms

This glossary provides brief definitions of key concepts used throughout the book, offering clarity for both practitioners and readers new to the fields of neuroscience, trauma-informed care, and somatic healing.

Attachment Wounds
Disruptions or injuries in early caregiver relationships that impair the development of secure emotional bonds, often shaping adult relational patterns and nervous system responses.

Autonomic Nervous System (ANS)
A division of the peripheral nervous system responsible for involuntary functions such as heart rate, digestion, and respiration. It includes the sympathetic, parasympathetic, and enteric branches.

Bottom-Up Regulation
The process of influencing brain function and emotional state through body-based (somatic) input, such as breath, posture, and sensory stimuli.

Co-Regulation
The reciprocal process by which nervous systems regulate each other through presence, eye contact, vocal tone, rhythm, and attunement.

Dissociation
A disconnection between thoughts, emotions, body sensations, or identity, often occurring in response to overwhelming stress or trauma as a protective mechanism.

Dorsal Vagal State
A state of parasympathetic nervous system dominance associated with immobilization, shutdown, numbness, or collapse. Common in individuals with chronic trauma.

Embodiment
The practice of fully inhabiting one's physical body with awareness, presence, and responsiveness. It involves connecting to internal sensations (interoception) and external orientation (exteroception).

Fawn Response
A lesser-known trauma response characterized by appeasing, people-pleasing, or self-abandonment in an effort to maintain safety in relationships.

Hypervigilance
A state of persistent nervous system arousal marked by heightened alertness, scanning for danger, and difficulty relaxing—even in the absence of threat.

Interoception
The capacity to perceive internal body sensations, such as hunger, heart rate, breath, or gut feelings. It is essential for emotional awareness and self-regulation.

Neurosomatic Intelligence (NSI)
An applied framework that integrates neuroscience, somatic practices, and trauma-informed care to restore nervous system capacity, regulation, and resilience.

Polyvagal Theory
A model developed by Dr. Stephen Porges that explains how the vagus nerve influences emotional regulation, social engagement, and physiological states of safety and threat.

Reparenting
A process in which individuals offer themselves the nurturing, boundaries, and support they did not receive in early caregiving relationships.

Somatic Practice

A body-centered therapeutic or experiential method that emphasizes the role of the nervous system, physical sensation, and movement in healing and transformation.

State Before Strategy
A core NSI principle that emphasizes regulating the nervous system before attempting cognitive or behavioral change.

Sympathetic Nervous System
A branch of the ANS responsible for mobilization, stress response, and activation—commonly associated with "fight or flight" responses.

Titration
A trauma-informed approach that introduces healing stimuli or experiences in small, manageable doses to avoid overwhelming the system.

Vagal Tone
An indicator of parasympathetic nervous system health and flexibility, related to one's ability to recover from stress and engage socially.

Appendix B: Neurosomatic Intelligence (NSI) Principles

Neurosomatic Intelligence (NSI) is a trauma-informed, body-based framework that supports nervous system regulation, resilience, and reconnection. These principles serve as the foundation for nervous system healing, supporting both practitioners and clients in cultivating embodied transformation.

1. State Before Strategy

Before implementing cognitive tools or behavioral change, we must assess and regulate the current nervous system state. Safety, not logic, is the prerequisite for change.

> **Application:** Regulation precedes reflection. When dysregulated, the body must be soothed before the mind can process.

2. The Body is the Storykeeper

Trauma lives in the body, not just in memory. NSI recognizes the body as the narrator of one's lived experience and healing requires listening somatically.

> **Application:** Movement, posture, gesture, and sensation provide insight into unresolved survival responses.

3. Behavior is State-Dependent

All behavior—whether adaptive or self-sabotaging—is rooted in nervous system state. NSI reframes resistance or reactivity as protective responses rather than personal failings.

> **Application:** Practitioners track shifts in physiology (tone, breath, eye contact, posture) to understand what the system is communicating.

4. Survival Responses Are Intelligent

Freeze, flight, fight, and fawn are not dysfunctions—they are the nervous system's way of preserving safety. NSI honors these patterns as once-intelligent, even if they are no longer necessary.

> **Application:** Rather than pathologizing survival states, we support the completion and integration of incomplete protective responses.

5. Regulation Is Relational

The nervous system co-regulates with other humans and with the environment. Healing is amplified through attuned presence, rhythm, and resonance.

> **Application:** Practitioners prioritize their own regulation to become safe co-regulators for others.

6. Safety Is Felt, Not Told

Telling someone they are safe does not make them feel safe. Safety must be experienced through predictable, gentle, and consistent somatic cues.

> **Application:** Use tone, breath, pacing, and environment to send cues of safety to the brainstem.

7. Healing Requires Capacity Building

Trauma narrows capacity; healing widens it. NSI supports titrated expansion—adding sensation, emotion, and complexity at a pace the body can integrate.

> **Application:** The goal is not comfort, but capacity—to tolerate more sensation without overwhelm.

8. The Body Learns Through Repetition

Neural plasticity requires repetition. Consistent somatic practices lay the groundwork for new neural pathways to take root and strengthen over time.

Application: Encourage small, frequent practices rather than intense one-time interventions.

9. Expression Is a Function of Safety

Authentic voice, emotion, and creativity emerge when the nervous system feels safe. NSI teaches that suppression is not a flaw, but a survival adaptation.

Application: Practices like vocal toning, mirror work, and movement expression rebuild permission to be fully seen and heard.

10. Transformation Is Bottom-Up

Lasting change emerges from bottom-up processes—regulation, co-regulation, interoception—not just top-down insight. NSI shifts the focus from forceful change to embodied integration.

Application: Transformation is not forced from the mind—it is earned through safety in the body.

Appendix C: Practitioner Tools & Protocols

Quick-Reference Somatic Practices, Nervous System Drills, and Co-Regulation Techniques

This appendix provides a curated collection of trauma-informed, neuroscience-based tools designed to support both practitioners and clients in the application of Neurosomatic Intelligence (NSI). These practices can be used to facilitate regulation, deepen interoceptive awareness, increase capacity for emotional resilience, and cultivate sustainable healing.

I. Somatic Practices for Self-Regulation

1. Orienting to Safety

- *Purpose*: Decrease hypervigilance; support parasympathetic engagement.

- *Instructions*: Slowly scan the room or environment with your eyes. Pause to name three safe or familiar objects, textures, or colors. Breathe slowly while orienting.

- *Nervous System Target*: Reduces sympathetic arousal, enhances vagal tone.

2. Grounding Through Touch

- *Purpose*: Interrupt dissociation and support present-moment awareness.

- *Instructions*: Place one hand on the chest and one on the belly. Apply gentle pressure. Breathe deeply into the contact. Name sensations: warmth, weight, texture.

- *Modification*: Hold a weighted object or textured item.

- *Nervous System Target*: Increases somatosensory

engagement, supports prefrontal cortex activation.

3. Extended Exhale Breathing
- *Purpose*: Activate the parasympathetic branch of the autonomic nervous system.

- *Instructions*: Inhale for 4 counts, exhale slowly for 6–8 counts. Repeat for 3–5 minutes.

- *Clinical Use*: Helps with sleep prep, panic attacks, or high arousal states.

4. Vagal Toning Through Sound
- *Purpose*: Stimulate vagus nerve and improve emotional regulation.

- *Instructions*: Engage in low-pitched humming, OM chanting, or singing. Focus on the vibration in the throat, chest, and jaw.

- *Nervous System Target*: Enhances limbic system modulation and vagal pathways.

II. Nervous System Drills

These drills are designed to build nervous system capacity, improve interoception and proprioception, and support regulation by enhancing neural efficiency. NSI-based drills are most effective when titrated, practiced consistently, and paired with tracking tools such as a nervous system journal or pre/post-sensation check-ins.

1. Trigeminal Nerve Stimulation (Facial Neuromuscular Activation)
- **Purpose**: Regulate autonomic arousal; soften defensive facial patterns; increase vagal tone.

- **Instructions**: Gently rub or tap around the eyes, jawline, and forehead using slow, circular motion. Pair with humming or light facial movements (eyebrow lifts, cheek puckers).

- **Clinical Application**: Use for clients experiencing social withdrawal, vocal suppression, or shutdown.

2. **Ocular-Vestibular Reset (Visual-Vestibular Recalibration)**
   - **Purpose**: Reorient dysregulated vestibular input and visual tracking; support re-integration post-dissociation.

   - **Instructions**: While standing or seated, hold a finger in front of the face. Slowly track the finger with the eyes (not head) left to right, then up and down. Repeat for 30 seconds per direction.

   - **Enhancement**: Add head movement opposite to the finger movement for additional challenge.

   - **Clinical Application**: Use with clients showing signs of disorientation, light sensitivity, or sensory overwhelm.

3. **Cross-Lateral Patterning (Bilateral Integration)**
   - **Purpose**: Integrate left and right brain hemispheres; support regulation and coherence.

   - **Instructions**: March in place while alternately tapping the opposite knee or shoulder (left hand to right knee, right hand to left knee). Add rhythmic vocalizations or count aloud.

   - **Duration**: 1–2 minutes.

   - **Clinical Application**: Helpful for clients experiencing racing thoughts, overwhelm, or freeze responses.

4. Interoceptive Tracking Drill

- **Purpose**: Enhance awareness of internal cues (hunger, tension, breath, heartbeat).

- **Instructions**: Pause, close eyes, and ask the body:
  - "Where do I feel most sensation right now?"
  - "What is the temperature, pressure, or rhythm there?"
  - "If this sensation had a message, what would it say?"

- **Clinical Application**: Excellent for clients with alexithymia, dissociation, or mind-body disconnect.

5. Tongue Position Reset (Cranial Nerve Rebalancing)

- **Purpose**: Realign cranial nerve tension that affects breath, jaw tension, and vagal tone.

- **Instructions**: Gently press the tongue to the roof of the mouth (soft palate), keeping the jaw relaxed. Breathe slowly through the nose for 1–2 minutes.

- **Clinical Application**: Can be used to reset after a session, manage overwhelm, or support somatic safety in speech-related trauma.

III. Co-Regulation Techniques

These techniques support nervous system regulation through safe, attuned connection with others. Co-regulation is not about fixing—it is about being present, regulated, and resonant in a way that invites the other person's system toward safety and stability.

1. Matching and Mirroring

- **Purpose**: Establish attunement by syncing breath, posture, tone, or movement.

- **Instructions**: Observe your client's current rhythm (e.g., breathing pace, body position). Slowly begin to mirror this, then gradually shift your own rhythm toward calm and grounded. The client's system may follow without verbal prompting.

- **Clinical Use**: Useful in the beginning of sessions to build safety or reconnect after rupture or dissociation.

2. Rhythmic Regulation with Breath

- **Purpose**: Use breath as a shared regulatory tool.

- **Instructions**: Breathe audibly and slowly while maintaining soft presence and non-directive eye contact (if appropriate). Invite the client to "breathe with you" or simply allow them to unconsciously match your tempo.

- **Optional**: Pair with soft verbal cues like, "Let's settle together," or "We're just breathing now."

- **Clinical Use**: For clients in sympathetic arousal, panic, or agitation.

3. Co-Holding Somatic Anchors

- **Purpose**: Use shared physical cues to support containment and presence.

- **Instructions**: Each person holds their own body part (e.g., placing a hand on heart, belly, or shoulders). Reflect on internal sensations together. "Notice what happens when we both place our hands here."

- **Clinical Use**: Effective during trauma processing or when grounding is needed during emotional activation.

4. Voice as Regulation

- **Purpose**: Use tone, cadence, and volume of your voice to cue safety.

- **Instructions**: Speak in a low, slow, and prosodic tone. Avoid abrupt changes in pitch or volume. Use short, validating phrases such as:

    - "I'm right here with you."

    - "You're doing beautifully."

    - "Let's stay with that together."

- **Clinical Use**: Soothes clients in hyperaroused or dissociative states; deepens presence.

5. Grounding in Parallel

- **Purpose**: Model and mirror grounding techniques with the client.

- **Instructions**: While the client watches, name aloud your current grounding resource (e.g., "I'm feeling my feet pressing into the floor."). Invite them to try and share what they notice.

- **Optional Add-On**: Use dual grounding tools (weighted blankets, textured objects, bilateral stimulation) while staying in connection.

- **Clinical Use**: Reorients clients to the present moment and supports interoceptive connection through shared attention.

6. Titrated Touch (When Appropriate and Consented)

- **Purpose**: Use safe, attuned, and ethical touch as a regulatory anchor.

- **Instructions**: With full consent and discussion, place a hand on the client's shoulder, back, or hand as a grounding anchor.

- **Clinical Use**: Only with clients who have built strong safety and somatic awareness. Touch should always be client-directed and never used for emotional containment without permission.

Appendix D: Nervous System States Chart

Nervous System State	Polyvagal Branch	Physical Sensations	Emotional Tone	Behavioral Patterns	Somatic Cues & NSI Tools
Ventral Vagal (Safety & Social Engagement)	Parasympathetic	Steady breath, relaxed muscles, open posture	Calm, connected, curious	Engaged, expressive, open to connection	Eye contact, humming, co-regulation, breath pacing
Sympathetic (Mobilization: Fight or Flight)	Sympathetic	Increased heart rate, muscle tension, shallow breath	Anxious, angry, restless	Hypervigilance, controlling, reactive	Shaking, paced exhale, grounding through movement
Dorsal Vagal (Shutdown/Freeze)	Parasympathetic (immobilization)	Numbness, heavy limbs, slowed breathing, collapsed posture	Numb, disconnected, despairing	Withdrawal, shutdown, immobilized	Gentle rocking, warmth, light movement, soft sound
Blended: Functional Freeze	Sympathetic + Dorsal	Frozen outside, activated inside; stillness with tension	Overwhelmed, stuck, confused	Masking, dissociation, fawning	Titration, orienting, containment (e.g. self-hold)
Fawn (Appease/People-Pleasing)	Survival adaptation (learned)	Muscle bracing, holding breath, tight jaw	Anxious, overly accommodating	Over-apologizing, over-giving, conflict-avoidant	Somatic boundaries, voice activation, self-touch anchoring

Appendix E: Daily Practice Templates

Integrating Neurosomatic Intelligence (NSI) Into Daily Life

These ample templates support nervous system regulation through consistent, embodied routines. Use them for personal integration or with clients as part of careplans.

1. Morning Regulation Ritual

Practice	Instructions
Breath Check-In	3 rounds of box breathing (4-4-4-4) or 4-7-8 breath
Sensory Anchoring	Identify 3 things you see, 2 you hear, 1 you feel (orienting practice)
Body Mapping	Scan for areas of tension, numbness, or sensation and name what you notice
Micro-Movement	Gentle stretch, sway, or shake to awaken interoception
Set a Regulation Intention	"Today I will return to my body when I feel ___." (fill in with a stress cue)

2. Midday Reset Plan

Practice	Instructions
Vagal Toning	Hum, sing, or chant softly for

	60 seconds
Self-Contact	Apply pressure to chest, arms, or legs with slow exhale (e.g., butterfly tap or self-hug)
Refocus With Senses	Run hands under cold water or use essential oil for a sensory shift
Recalibrate with Breath	2-minute extended exhale (e.g., 4 in / 6 out)
Grounding Prompt	"What does my nervous system need right now—movement, stillness, or support?"

3. Evening Reflection and Wind-Down
Duration: 10–20 minutes

Practice	Instructions
Somatic Journaling Prompt	"What did my body teach me today?" or "Where did I override my cues?"
Gratitude Scan	Name 3 things your body helped you do today
Downshift Breath	5–10 minutes of diaphragmatic breathing with hands on belly
Weighted Support	Use a blanket or pillow for proprioceptive comfort while seated or lying down
Sleep Cue Setting	Visualize or verbally affirm safety: "It is safe to rest. I am

supported."

4. Personalized Micro-Regulation Plan

Situation	Somatic Cue	Practice	Support
Conflict with partner	Jaw tension, racing heart	Grounding + breath pacing	Ask for pause and space
Work overwhelm	Shoulders raised, shallow breath	Standing shake + exhale	Brief movement break
Emotional shutdown	Numbness, foggy head	Self-contact + sound (hum)	Step outside for sensory reset

Appendix F: Recommended Reading & Resources

For Practitioners, Students, and Healing-Centered Readers

Books: Trauma, Neuroscience & Somatic Healing

- **Bessel van der Kolk (2014)** – *The Body Keeps the Score: Brain, Mind, and Body in the Healing of Trauma*

- **Peter Levine (1997)** – *Waking the Tiger: Healing Trauma*

- **Stephen Porges (2011)** – *The Polyvagal Theory: Neurophysiological Foundations of Emotions, Attachment, Communication, and Self-Regulation*

- **Deb Dana (2018)** – *The Polyvagal Theory in Therapy: Engaging the Rhythm of Regulation*

- **Gabor Maté (2008)** – *In the Realm of Hungry Ghosts: Close Encounters with Addiction*

- **Kristin Neff (2011)** – *Self-Compassion: The Proven Power of Being Kind to Yourself*

- **Arielle Schwartz (2020)** – *The Complex PTSD Workbook: A Mind-Body Approach to Regaining Emotional Control and Becoming Whole*

- **Diane Poole Heller (2019)** – *The Power of Attachment: How to Create Deep and Lasting Intimate Relationships*

- **Resmaa Menakem (2017)** – *My Grandmother's Hands: Racialized Trauma and the Pathway to Mending Our Hearts and Bodies*

- **Stephen Cope (2000)** – *Yoga and the Quest for the True Self*

Neurosomatic Intelligence & Applied Practices

- **Neurosomatic Intelligence Training** (NSI Certification Program): www.neurosomaticintelligence.com

- **Z-Health Neuro Training Systems** – Applied neurology and movement re-education: www.zhealtheducation.com

- **Rewire Therapy** – Trauma-informed somatic training for practitioners: www.rewiretherapy.net

- **Polyvagal Institute** – Advanced nervous system education and training: www.polyvagalinstitute.org

Peer-Reviewed Articles & Research

- Porges, S. W. (2007). *The polyvagal perspective*. Biological Psychology, 74(2), 116–143.

- Schore, A. N. (2012). *The Science of the Art of Psychotherapy*. Norton.

- Ogden, P., Minton, K., & Pain, C. (2006). *Trauma and the body: A sensorimotor approach to psychotherapy*. Norton.

- Cozolino, L. (2010). *The Neuroscience of Psychotherapy: Healing the Social Brain*. Norton.

Online Learning & Communities

- NICABM (National Institute for the Clinical Application of Behavioral Medicine)
  www.nicabm.com
  Courses on trauma, somatic work, attachment, and brain-based healing.

- **Embody Lab**

www.theembodylab.com
Trainings and summits on integrative, trauma-informed care.

- **Sounds True – Healing Trauma Programs**
  www.soundstrue.com
  Workshops with leading authors and experts in trauma, neuroscience, and spirituality.

- **Shamanic Healing & Integrative Medicine Books**
  Published by *The Shamanic Goddess, LLC* – Books by Dr. Deilen Michelle Villegas, Ph.D., including:
    - Reclaiming the Unspoken
    - Rooted In Wisdom: Holistic Herbalism for the Healing Communities
    - Beyond Chemistry: Hormones, Healing & Human Connection in the Age of Disconnection
    - Sacred Flesh: The Science, Spirit, and Power of Intimacy

Appendix G: Client Consent & Safety Practices

Guidelines for Trauma-Informed, Ethical Practice and NSI-Based Session Preparation

1. Foundational Principles of Ethical Practice

- **Do No Harm**: All somatic and NSI-based techniques must prioritize the client's autonomy, pace, and readiness.

- **Informed Consent**: Clients must be fully aware of what techniques, assessments, or tools will be used and must give verbal and/or written consent.

- **Confidentiality**: Clearly outline the boundaries of confidentiality and exceptions (e.g., harm to self/others, mandated reporting).

- **Scope of Practice**: Always work within your credentials, licensure, and training. Refer out when clinical issues are beyond your scope.

2. Informed Consent Template (Sample Language)

> "This session will include somatic and nervous system-based practices that focus on body awareness, breathwork, visualization, and movement. These practices are intended to support regulation, safety, and resilience, and are informed by Neurosomatic Intelligence (NSI) principles.
>
> You are invited to participate at your own pace, and you have the right to pause, opt out, or ask for clarification at any time. Nothing will be done without your consent."

Include a client signature section if using written consent.

3. NSI-Aligned Session Preparation

Before Session
- Regulate your own nervous system: Use a personal regulation ritual (breathwork, grounding, movement).
- Clarify client goals: What is the focus of the session? What is their current window of tolerance?
- Prepare a flexible framework: Always prioritize state over strategy.

During Session
- Begin with a check-in: "How's your body today? What's alive in your system right now?"
- Continuously seek permission: "Would you like to try a brief grounding exercise before we begin?"
- Track nervous system shifts: Look for signs of up-regulation, freeze, collapse, or fawning.

After Session
- Offer integration tools: Encourage hydration, journaling, or a sensory reset (e.g., feet on ground, warm tea).
- Normalize delayed processing: "Sometimes insights or emotions arise after the session. That's okay and expected."

4. Client Safety & Regulation Protocols
- **Red Flags to Pause/Stop**:
    - Dissociation or glassy-eyed stare

- Breath holding or shallow panic breathing
- Collapse in posture or loss of verbal engagement
- Emotional flooding beyond the window of tolerance

- **Interventions to Re-Establish Safety:**
  - Orienting exercises (look around the room slowly, name what you see)
  - Bilateral stimulation (tapping shoulders/knees alternately)
  - Gentle vocalization (humming, long vowel sounds)
  - Physical grounding (hold a weighted object or press feet into the floor)

5. Client Agreements & Boundaries

- Sessions are collaborative—not hierarchical.
- The client is always the expert of their own body.
- Safety includes honoring **"No"** as much as **"Yes"**.
- Homework or between-session practices should never be mandatory or overwhelming.

6. Feedback & Ongoing Consent

Build a regular feedback loop:
- "What felt helpful or not helpful today?"
- "Is there anything you'd like to revisit or do differently

next time?"

This cultivates trust, transparency, and mutual respect over time.

Appendix H: Acknowledgments

Gratitude, Collaboration, and the Legacy Behind the Work

To arrive at the completion of this book is not a solitary accomplishment—it is the culmination of years of witnessing, listening, unlearning, remembering, and becoming. It is woven from the wisdom of countless teachers, sacred traditions, clients, ancestors, and lived experiences that have shaped my practice and deepened my purpose.

To My Ancestors

Thank you for the resilience, the rituals, and the remembrance. For your songs whispered through herbs, prayers, and dreams. This work is offered as a continuation of your legacy and a vow to never let our medicine be forgotten.

To My Clients

You are the heartbeat of this work. Thank you for your courage to return to the body, to feel the unfelt, to speak the unspoken. Every breakthrough, every trembling breath, every sacred pause has taught me more than any textbook ever could. You remind me that healing is possible—and contagious.

To My Mentors and Educators

To those who have guided me in neuroscience, trauma studies, somatics, and sacred traditions—thank you for challenging me to integrate rigor with reverence. Your teachings helped me birth a model that honors both science and soul.

Special thanks to the community of **Neurosomatic Intelligence practitioners and educators** who continue to innovate in the field of trauma-informed healing and nervous system science.

To My Collaborators

Thank you to the editors, researchers, thought partners,

and co-dreamers who shaped this manuscript and supported its vision from conception to completion. Your belief in this work helped me stay grounded in moments of doubt and lifted me when I felt alone.

To My Family

To my husband, children, and chosen family—thank you for your patience, love, and steady presence. You are my reason and my reminder. Your support allowed me to pour my whole self into this work without losing sight of who I am.

To the Future Practitioners and Readers

You are part of this living legacy. Thank you for saying yes to this work, to yourself, and to the sacred task of healing in a world that often forgets how. May these words inspire not just understanding, but embodiment.

With deep reverence and revolutionary hope,
Dr. Deilen Michelle Villegas, Ph.D.
The Shamanic Goddess

www.ingramcontent.com/pod-product-compliance
Lightning Source LLC
Chambersburg PA
CBHW060834190426
43197CB00039B/2583